God and Harry Potter at Yale

*Teaching Faith and Fantasy Fiction
in an Ivy League Classroom*

The Rev. Danielle Elizabeth Tumminio

For information, contact Unlocking Press
www.UnlockingPress.com

Unlocking Press titles may be purchased for business or promotional use or special sales.
Unless indicated otherwise, Scripture is taken from the New Revised Standard Version of the Bible, copyright 1989 by the Division of Christian Education of the National Council of Churches in the United States of America. All rights reserved.

Cover Design by Joyce Odell
Back Cover photo copyright Julie Carlson
10 - 9 - 8 - 7 - 6 - 5 - 4 - 3 - 2 - 1

nlocking
press
www.UnlockingPress.com

0-9829633-1-9

978-0-9829633-1-9

DEDICATION:

To Dad, who encouraged a love of God.

To Mom, who introduced me to Harry.

And to Marilyn, my teacher since I
arrived at Yale.

Table of Contents

CHAPTER 1

Introductions on the First Day of Class

In the Beginning

I WROTE THE BOOK in your hands because of quotations like this: "Let me say something about Harry Potter. Warlocks are enemies of God. And I don't care what kind of hero they are, they're an enemy of God, and had it been in the Old Testament, Harry Potter would have been put to death. You don't make heroes out of warlocks."[1] Youth minister Becky Fischer preached this to children attending the famous summer program documented in *Jesus Camp*, and many of these young people took her words to heart not only because she was a spiritual authority, but also because her beliefs are dominant in many Christian households today.

Are objections like Becky Fischer's warranted? This book aims to respond to this question by exploring whether the message of *Harry Potter* constitutes a Christian heresy. I hope that this book will also deal with a fundamental error in the way Christians have analyzed Rowling's writing. In the past, discussion about Christianity's influence on the series focused primarily on witchcraft, and while there is some merit to considering the morality of wands and witches, this topic has

---

1   *Jesus Camp*, dir. Heidi Ewing and Rachel Grady, perf. Becky Fischer, 2007.

monopolized what ought to be a much broader debate.

The problem with evaluating the merit of the *Harry Potter* series only using witchcraft is that Christianity has more to it than just a moral stance on magic. Put differently, one cannot draw conclusions based on a single topic when dealing with such an extensive faith tradition. It would be like reading only a single chapter from a multi-volume set of novels and assuming you knew what they were about, like reading only the first-third of *Breaking Dawn* or the latter half of *The Golden Compass*. Just as perusing such a small selection from those stories wouldn't give you a true sense of the series of which they are a part, so engaging with only one topic from Christianity is not enough to prove that the books are heretical.

As a result of these previous dialogues, you will see very little about witchcraft here. Other authors have already discussed this topic in great detail and I see no need to rehash old news. Instead, we will be discussing those themes that have been mostly overlooked: topics such as evil, sin, salvation, grace, and the end times. Christianity has a rich history of thought on these topics, a history that has not received the attention it ought to in this arena. So together we will explore the most prominent themes of a two thousand-year-old faith that has captured the hearts of billions. As we encounter each topic, we will ask the following question: "What does Christianity say about this idea, and what does *Harry Potter* say about it?"

My hypothesis throughout this book is that the series *does* resonate with the Christian worldview, but often these resonances occur in unexpected ways. You may walk away from this book disagreeing with this theory or still believing that the series is heretical, and if so, that is fine. But I ask that you do so with an informed mind. That is the rigor I demand of my students and the rigor I will ask of you as a reader, but perhaps most importantly, it is the respect both the *Harry Potter* books and Christianity deserve.

Introductions

Before we turn to details about my class at Yale or heated discussions about faith and fiction, I'd like to tell you a little bit about myself so you know something about who wrote the words on your page. It seems like Christianity captured my spirit at birth. I would drag my parents—who were not particularly religious—into any church we passed, and as a toddler, barely able to express myself, I told them to stop speaking to me because, "God was talking." Unfortunately, when they asked what God said, I announced that the conversation took place in Bethlehem and I had no details to share! They took me to church after that, and I remember spending my younger years sitting on a cushion in the aisle of our Episcopal congregation, mimicking the actions of the minister. When I was old enough to read, I joined the choir in the local cathedral, which rehearsed three days a week and gave me not only an incredible music education, but also a rich knowledge of the Bible. It was there that I first learned about the Trinity, the Eucharist, and what Christians thought about sin, and because of those hours singing, verses from Scripture are etched deep in my being.

Growing up, I also had a love of literature, so when I began my undergraduate years at Yale, I continued to think about faith, but I decided to be an English major. When I graduated, I moved about a mile uphill to the Divinity School campus, where I spent five years earning two master's degrees, devouring texts on theology, and cultivating the art of being a poor graduate student. I also entered an Episcopal ordination process, decided to get a PhD in theology and violence, became a spinning instructor, did a lot of yoga, sang in a professional choir, and got the idea for a class on *Harry Potter* and the Christian faith that would eventually turn into this book.

Crafting the Class

This work originated in the attic where I lived during my graduate school years at Yale. In exchange for grocery shopping, cooking, and kitchen cleaning, I lived rent-free above two professors in a cozy apartment with sloped ceilings, an antique bathtub with feet, and a sometimes-leaky roof. It could be hot in the summer and cold in the winter, but the professors were kind, and living in an attic felt artistic to me, even though the dust bothered my allergies.

.   Torrential rains poured outside the night my two friends, Matt and Kat, came over to help me strategize about a project that had been developing in the recesses of my brain: teaching a college seminar at Yale. The College Seminar program is a unique institution that offers classes for undergraduates through the residential colleges, which are like houses at Hogwarts, only there are 12 of them. Some mysterious force or person in the Admissions Office assigns freshmen to a college—Yale's version of the sorting hat—and students then spend the next four years living there. Though they exist primarily for housing and dining, the colleges also have classrooms that house one or two courses per term.

It's not easy to get a teaching post in the program. An application goes through a rigorous process in which it is reviewed by each college. If one or more colleges like the proposal, then the applicant gets an interview, and after all the interviews are completed, the colleges decide which courses will be sponsored. If a proposal makes it to this stage, it must then pass through all the other bureaucratic channels at Yale before being given a green light.

One thing that is unique about the program is that it is designed to give non-faculty members the opportunity to teach, provided that they are upper level graduate students at Yale or successful professionals in their field. I knew it was hard to get approval as a graduate student, but I thought I'd give it a shot with an idea I'd been mulling around for awhile: a semester-long seminar on *Harry Potter* and Christian thought.

It seemed like the perfect fit for me. I had an undergraduate degree in English literature, a master's in Christian theology, and I loved the books. I'd followed the heated debate about whether the books were heretical with the kind of enthusiasm that 7-year-old girls have for Hannah Montana. At a gut level, I felt like these critics were missing something crucial in the series by focusing on witchcraft when there was so much more to Christian thought than just that one topic. There was love and death, sacrifice and salvation, creation and sin, resurrection and grace, to name just a few. If Christians really wanted to know whether the *Harry Potter* books were antithetical to their faith, then they needed to consider what the series said about *all* of these topics, not just one. And they needed to do it in a sustained way…say over an entire academic term.

I also thought that using the *Harry Potter* books as a vehicle to teach theology might attract students who otherwise wouldn't turn to the religious studies section of the course catalogue. I'd heard many Yalies—including some in my graduate program—lamenting the thought of theology classes. Non-Christians said the topics weren't relevant to them, and seminarians felt they were too abstract to relate to parish life. This struck me as unfortunate because even for a non-Christian, the kinds of questions theologians ask are personal and pressing, in other words, anything but abstract and irrelevant.

Moreover, the irony is that human beings ponder theological questions all the time. A child might wonder why God allowed his father to die or a banker might debate whether to give change to a homeless man. Behind these everyday dilemmas lies the heart of theology, and yet despite the fact many people think about these things, few of them enroll in formal courses. It's a bizarre dichotomy: the questions that help people find meaning in real life feel irrelevant in the classroom. So I hoped to make theology more interesting by bringing real life to the classroom and asking students whether the *Harry Potter* books espoused a Christian worldview.

The trouble was that this was all just a glimmer in my head, and while I had some sense of direction for the course, the finer details of the relationship between the books and Christianity was still an amorphous brain blob. Hence, Matt and Kat. This rhyming duo was my Ron and Hermione, my Willow and Xander, my Jimmy Olsen and Lois Lane. In short, they were dear friends. Ever since we were undergraduates, the three of us had calmed each other's neuroses, sang together in choirs, traveled to theme parks, talked about faith, laughed 'til we shed tears, and played crossword puzzles. Although, truth be told, it was only Matt and Kat who did the crosswords— Matt would dutifully fill in the blocks he knew and Kat would make up words for answers she didn't, which inevitably made Matt scratch his head and say things like, "Emblist is a word?"

But on this rainy evening, crossword puzzles were replaced by seven *Harry Potter* books and a host of Christian theology texts, all of them battling for space with the Pepe's pizza box on my kitchen table. Kat, whose brown curls made her look like a Grecian goddess, and Matt, whose wit could soften even a curmudgeon like Simon Cowell, were strategizing about what topics to cover in which class. We started with the rough list of those I'd developed and then the three of us brainstormed, using our combined backgrounds in religion and literature.

"I wonder if Azkaban could be Rowling's equivalent of Hell," Matt said. "And if so, that could make for a really interesting discussion about damnation."

"Oh my gosh, yes," Kat chimed in. "And you know what else you could do with that? You could talk about how the Pure Bloods are kind of like a perverse elect. And then you could talk about whether it makes sense theologically if the Devil has an elected body just like Calvinist Christianity does."

And so the hours passed by. The three of us exchanged ideas until our minds were sore. The rain stopped, and we traded pizza for ice cream, and by the end of the evening, I had a syllabus.

I spent the next week revising, altering, and proofreading the application before turning in 12 copies (about 120 pages of text) to the College Seminar office. Then I waited and tried to forget about the application so I wouldn't be disappointed if I didn't get an interview. About six weeks later, just as I'd nearly wiped the idea of teaching the course from my mind, I received an e-mail from Branford College. Then came ones from Trumbull, Silliman, and Morse. In interview after interview, I met this challenging question, "Could you fill a whole semester with this?" That was the most common objection I encountered during the proposal process. I tried to explain to the interviewers that in most ways, this was a theology class, a kind of spoon-full-of-sugar way of teaching a topic that many students didn't think to study. Members of the class would be assigned 150-200 pages of theology reading each week, and they would touch upon some of the most complicated historical and contemporary thinkers in Christianity. This was a hefty reading load, considering they also had about 250 pages of *Harry Potter* to get through.

Moreover, the Christian belief system wasn't something that could be taught in an hour or two. It has a two thousand year history with ideas that have preoccupied the entire careers of philosophers, priests, and faithful believers. These individuals had spent ages searching for answers to theological questions that might explain their world in a more meaningful way. In light of this, the question in my mind was not whether the class could fill thirteen weeks but whether thirteen weeks could be enough.

I came home from each interview uncertain about whether I'd convinced the committee that a class like this could be a success, and shortly after finishing them, I received a brief e-mail from Kat that confirmed my suspicions. "Have you seen this article?" she wrote. "Thought you'd want to take a look."

I opened up the link to see an article in the *Yale Daily News* titled, "For seminar selection, Potter will have to wait." It began like this:

> Despite the Hogwartian allure of Yale's Gothic-style colleges, Muggle undergraduates may have to look elsewhere to catch a true glimpse of the magical world of Harry Potter....
>
> Peter Luehring-Jones '09, co-chair of the Saybrook committee, said Saybrook begins each semester with about 40 proposals, which are winnowed down to 15 before the interview stage. He said he doubts dragons and Hogwarts will enter Yale's hallowed halls any time soon.
>
> "The committee had a good laugh over the Harry Potter proposal," Luehring-Jones said. "It had a really well-written introduction that made it sound very interesting, but not something that you could talk about for 13 weeks."[2]

My initial reaction was to sigh, then laugh, then lament the media, and then be sad. Saybrook hadn't offered an interview, so

2   Patrick Lee, "For seminar selection, Potter will have to wait," 7 10 2007, *Yale Daily News*, 20 08 2009 <http://www.yaledailynews.com/articles/view/22107>.

it was no surprise that they wouldn't be hosting the class, and yet I wondered, "Is this what everyone I interviewed with thought? Did the colleges that interviewed me only do so to catch a glimpse of the eccentric person who thought this was a good idea?"

And then, in a truly *Deus ex machina* moment, the acceptance e-mails came, first from Branford College and then from Trumbull.

Saybrook sponsored the class the following year.

The Students

Seventy-nine students showed up for the first day of class. They crowded into the Branford College seminar room, and when it filled to capacity, they streamed into the courtyard. The crowd was so extensive that by the time I arrived I had a hard time getting through the door myself. Because only 18 students were allowed to enroll in the course, those present had to fill out an application form with standard information, such as their year and residential college, along with a statement of interest.

I am reasonably certain that no other instructor at Yale has ever read applications like the ones I received. There were photographs of students dressed in Hogwarts robes at midnight book releases, Gryffindor crests watermarked onto the application cards, and stories about how Neville Longbottom was the topic of their admissions essay. The potential members of my class had created Quidditch Clubs and Harry Potter service groups; they had won essay contests, met J.K. Rowling, and attended fan conventions. One of them wrote, "I know I'm a freshman and it would take an act of magic to get into this class, but Harry was the underdog, and so I figured that if he could beat all the odds, maybe I could too."

But what struck me most about the words on their cards was the way in which Harry and his world had shaped their childhoods. The only freshman admitted to the course said in her application that she read the first book in fourth grade and the final installment came out her senior year of high school. Another student described the books as her "rainy day friends," a term that has stayed with me ever since. These Yalies were the first generation of young people to grow up alongside the *Harry Potter* series, and the books were an important part of their development. For some, Cedric's murder was their first exposure to death; for others, Hermione's tears over Ron were their introduction to heartbreak.

When I finally assembled a group, it was a diverse one. My class of 18 included a Hindu educated in Roman Catholic schools, a secular Jew, a Kenyan Episcopalian, a Mormon and a Southern Baptist, a smattering of Methodists, and an agnostic young woman from China, among others. It was the kind of diversity that I thought J.K. Rowling would approve of, the kind you would see in Hogwarts, unintentional but a gift. The enthusiasm in the class was infectious, and oftentimes nearly everyone would have their hands raised to talk, which is an image most people teaching in college would find unbelievable. They also quoted *Harry Potter* almost as seriously as Christians recite the Bible.

Which brings me to the Bible. I knew at the outset that 79 Yalies didn't apply for my class because they loved Christianity. Of course, some of them did—there were a handful of religious studies majors and a couple of faithful Christians who could recite Scripture verbatim, including chapter and verse. But my sense was that for many of my students, questions of faith were not particularly relevant to their lives.

This was something I hoped to fix by encouraging them to engage in discussions about different faith-based ideas. I did not aspire to convert them to Christianity, but I did hope to persuade them to believe that the questions a theological mind asks — questions such as, "What happens when we die?" or "Where is God in my experience of evil?" — are crucial and life-giving because they provide us with a deeper understanding of our world. We began to ask those questions at the very first class meeting, and I will begin with you where I began with them, with some introductions to theology and *Harry Potter*.

Theology, God, and Love in *Harry Potter*

- ### Defining Theology

Human beings have asked questions about the Christian faith for over two thousand years, questions like: Who is

God? What is Jesus all about? How does the Holy Spirit work in the world? What role does the Divine play in human life? As these questions grew increasingly complex, they fell into their own subject areas and were codified under the heading "theology." This term comes from the Greek *theologia*. In Greek, *theo-* means God and *–logia* means discourse, so *theologia* literally translates to something like God-talk or God-speak.

What makes theology such a challenging discipline is that it's hard to fit ideas together. Evil is the best example of this. In the entirety of Christian history, no one has been successful at developing a perfect reason why God would allow evil. Here's what I mean: imagine that I was having a conversation with a faithful Christian named Jane. Suppose I told Jane that God allowed evil because God wanted to punish people. She would probably respond that plenty of people experience evil who didn't do anything wrong. If I suggested that God allowed evil because humans could learn from negative experiences, Jane might object that some people who experience an evil die before they can learn anything, like those in car crashes. If I caved and then said, "Fine. Then there's no God," then Jane, because she is a Christian, would say, "But the Bible says there is." (When we get to the Revelation chapter, we'll see why it would be highly unlikely that Jane would dismiss the Bible's authority if she's a Christian.) Now, suppose I'm absolutely at my wits end and I say, "Well, maybe the things we think are evil just aren't. Maybe it's our perception," then Jane would probably conclude with something like, "But the suffering of billions stares us all in the face. Our experience of that is too overwhelming to be an illusion."[3]

From this simple example, you can see how complicated it is to make all the pieces of this logic puzzle fit together. It gets even more complicated when we try to make one topic cohesive with others, like aligning sin and evil or sacrifice and grace. So it becomes the goal of any theologian to make as much logical sense as possible, all the while recognizing that any framework

---

3   Most mainstream Christian traditions believe that evil is a reality; however some denominations, including the Church of Christ Scientist, consider evil to be an illusion.

he or she proposes will have its flaws. My former professor Miroslav Volf once described this phenomenon by saying theology is like packing a suitcase: there is always more to pack than can fit inside. Recognizing what is inside and outside the suitcase is key when evaluating a theological idea. In this book, we will consider how these different ideas appear—or do not appear—in the *Harry Potter* series, and we will also be considering what gets left in and what gets discarded from the wizarding world's suitcase. So let's go ahead and start with a cornerstone of Christian theology: the identity of God.

• Defining God

One of the first topics that historic theologians considered is the Christian conception of God.. The traditional belief is that God has three inherent characteristics: God is all-knowing, all-powerful, and all-good. Sometimes the word omniscient is substituted for all-knowing; omnipotent for all-powerful; and omnibenevolent for all-good.

The idea of the Three 'O' God who is omnibenevolent, omniscient, and omnipotent comes from some of the earliest Christian writers, known as the patristic writers. There are several reasons why these writers fashioned the Three O God as a hallmark of Christian thought. First, power. The initial chapter of the Book of Genesis describes God as a Creator who fashioned the universe—everything from day and night to water and sky, stars and sun, plants, animals, and humans. For God to have created all of this, God needed to know what God was doing and needed to be powerful enough to do it.

Second, goodness and knowledge. God is understood as a kind of cosmic CEO in charge of creation. Since the universe is so complicated, God had to be able to understand and manage the organization in a positive manner. If God couldn't do that in a way that was good and knowledgeable, then there would be a tyrant running the universe that wouldn't be worth respecting, never mind worshipping.

Finally, why God had to be the best at all these things. The early Christian writers were particularly interested in bringing Greek philosophical thought into conversation with Jewish thought so that each might regard the other as valued and respectable. One of the ideas prominent in Greek philosophical thought was that there is a chain of being, which means that things come in varieties from good to better to best, kind of like there are Saturns, Infinitis, and Rolls Royce's. From this perspective, God has to be the best—the Rolls Royce, so to speak—because if something bettered God, then that something would be more deserving of the title. Hence, for God to be God, God has to be at the extreme of greatness— maximally powerful, knowing, and good.

• Finding God in *Harry Potter*

So, is there a figure like this in *Harry Potter*? This is one of the first questions I put to my class, and initial discussion usually circulates about Dumbledore. Dumbledore was supremely knowledgeable and always strove to love and care for his students. Yet, as the series progresses, it becomes harder to maintain Dumbledore's absolute goodness, power, or knowledge. At the end of book five, Dumbledore admitted that he made a mistake by not telling Harry about the prophecy earlier; hence, we find that Dumbledore was not all-knowing. In book seven, we learn of his poor judgment regarding his family, so no omnibenevolence either. And as his declining health in book six evidences, there are at least physical powers greater than his. It would seem, then, that Dumbledore is almost a red herring God—one that the reader is lead to trust and believe in— who ultimately turns out to be a wise but flawed mortal. These realizations lead one of my students to write a paper she referred to as "Dumbledore as a God figure...but only through book three."

There is another character, less obvious perhaps, that members of the class have also suggested as a potential God figure: Lily Potter. Lily's sacrifice was certainly all-good, the protective charm she placed on Harry made her seem both all-knowing and all-powerful, and her elusive character causes Harry to identify with her the way humans often identify with God—as simultaneously loving but distant.

Yet the trouble with Lily is that she is unable to solve the overarching problem in the books—evil—and that means that she lacks power. She dies in the process of protecting her son, and while her protective charm does preserve Harry from death at Voldemort's hands, it does so only for a time. Thereafter, she may be a motivating force in the defeat of evil, but she contributes to it only indirectly. That she does not defeat Voldemort shows the limits to her power and prevents her from being a stand-in for God. (We will return to Lily's lack of power in the chapters on Christology and sacrifice.)

Now, just because Dumbledore and Lily fail to qualify as God-like doesn't mean that the series is devoid of such a character. But where that figure is proves to be an elusive search. Harry makes far too many mistakes to be seen as divine stand-in, and his psychological need to go-it-alone often makes the reader wish Hogwarts had a school psychologist on hand. Hermione, while smart, is certainly not all-powerful or all-knowing, and neither is Ron. Lupin has moments of selfishness in book seven that preclude him from being understood as all-good; Snape certainly doesn't fit the bill; James comes off as too self-absorbed to be all-knowing; McGonagall, though sturdy, can be physically dominated and is prone to misunderstanding Harry, while Sirius is a bit of a letdown across the board.

I would like to suggest that if there is anything akin to a God-figure in the books, it does not appear in the guise of human flesh. Rather, the one thing with the power to defeat Voldemort's evil, the goodness to want to, and the knowing to guide the operation is love. It is love that ultimately motivates Lily and Harry's sacrificial actions, love that keeps Hermione and Ron at Harry's side, love that prompts Neville's nobility in book seven, and love that saves the wizarding world at the end of the series. In fact, Rowling makes a point of driving home again and again the importance of love as a binding power, a power greater than all others that has the capacity to save. Even in the first book, Dumbledore impresses the importance of Love on Harry, saying,

> Your mother died to save you. If there is one thing Voldemort cannot understand, it is love. He didn't realize that love as powerful as your mother's for you

leaves its own mark. Not a scar, no not a visible sign…to have been loved so deeply, even though the person who loved us is gone, will give us some protection forever. It is in your very skin. Quirrell, full of hatred, greed, and ambition, sharing his soul with Voldemort, could not touch you for this reason. It was agony to touch a person marked by something so good (SS, 299).

So, what does having love as a God-figure say about the theology of Harry's world? Two things come to mind. First, it's a very Christian interpretation of the Divine. It says in the Bible that, "God is love, and those who live in love live in God and God lives in them" (1 John 4:7-8). For the books to represent love as the Divine reinforces a point that Christianity itself drives home.

But perhaps more interestingly, the idea that God is a non-human abstraction represents many people's experiences of what divine-human interactions are like. As individuals, we know love exists because we feel its effects, not because we've ever seen it. Likewise for those who believe in God. Additionally, for many people God is hard to find, and once found, hard to maintain a relationship with. We often wish God had an address or a phone number; we wish God was straightforward, delivering answers to prayers in a timely and organized way. But God is none of those things—God surprises, intrigues, allures, and sometimes disappoints. For though many people do have an intimate relationship with the Divine, others struggle to locate God's presence in their lives and feel that comforting power in a consistent way. Similarly for love—it can be hard to find and harder to maintain, but just because we can't see or touch it daily doesn't mean that it isn't always there.

The idea that God is love in the series also resonates with the experience of a seeker who really struggles to find and maintain a relationship with God, who is constantly discovering the Divine in new and surprising places. A seeker is not someone with all the answers; it is someone with all the questions. I suspect that this is one of the reasons J. K. Rowling's books appeal to such a wide audience and part of what makes them such a powerful teaching tool. Very few of us, if any, have all the answers when it comes to faith. For most of us, faith is like climbing a mountain—there are turns and switchbacks. Sometimes we encounter a cliff so steep we wonder if we'll be able to climb it. But occasionally, between the clouds, we can see the peak, and that keeps us moving. So, by presenting a God figure that reveals itself gradually, that appears slowly over time, the books make an effort to show that God is both a very real presence and a very challenging one. In this way, they paint a depiction of the Divine that is both true to Christianity and in line with human experience. They also encourage the reader to see the Christian faith in a new, but still valid, light, one that is less dogmatic and more exploratory, one that is creative yet true.

Authorial Intention

Now might be a good time to ask whether J.K. Rowling intended any of this. That's a tough question, and one to which I do not presume to know the answer. But here are some facts that are important to consider when we ask the question. First, we know that Rowling lives in a primarily Christian culture, has heard Christian sermons, and been saturated with the basics of Christianity holidays like Christmas and Easter, that are fundamental to the culture of the United Kingdom. Moreover, there are two biblical quotations in the books: "For where your treasure is, there your heart will be also" and "The last enemy to be destroyed is death" (Matt. 6:21 and I. Cor. 15:26). The presence of these quotations shows that at some level, Rowling knew she was interacting with Christianity.

If we want more compelling evidence than that, we can look to interviews in which Rowling states that she attended church as a child and professes to be a Christian. In fact, when asked point blank about her religious beliefs in an interview, she said,

> Yes I am [a Christian]… which seems to offend the religious right far worse than if I said I thought there was no God. Every time I've been asked if I believe in God, I've said yes, because I do, but no one ever really

has gone any more deeply into it than that, and I have to say that does suit me, because if I talk too freely about that I think the intelligent reader, whether 10 or 60, will be able to guess what's coming in the books.[4]

A quotation like this certainly implies that Rowling not only is a Christian but also that she purposefully included Christian themes and plotlines into the series. And if we want even more evidence, consider this statement Rowling made to the *Edinburgh Student Newspaper* in 2008: "There was a Christian commentator who said that Harry Potter had been the Christian church's biggest missed opportunity. And I thought, there's someone who actually has their eyes open."[5]

In other words, Rowling seems to think that the way the Christian community has read her books—as heretical or dangerous to their faith—is a misreading. The task of this book will therefore be to see whether she is correct in her belief, and as you continue reading, you will be given the theological tools to make your own informed decision.

But returning to authorial intention, even though Rowling professes to be a Christian and even implies that Christian themes are purposefully included in her books, it is impossible to know what is intended and what is not. Even if Rowling gave an interview and said that the books are an allegory about human relationships with God, she could be fibbing, and if she denied the claim, that doesn't mean that these ideas weren't motivating her creative subconscious. The truth is that none of us can get inside the mind of an author to know what he or she intended at any given moment. J.K. Rowling's writings are no different. Despite the fact that she has answered hundreds of questions on topics substantial and minute, we as readers still don't know the depths of how her brain put those

4   Max Wyman, "You can lead a fool to a book but you can't make them think': Author has frank words for the religious right," The Vancouver Sun (British Columbia), October 26, 2000 ," 2006, *Accio Quote, the Largest Archive of J.K. Rowling Interviews on the Web,* 10 1 2010 <http://www.accio-quote.org/articles/2000/1000-vancouversun-wyman.htm>.

5   Adeel Amini, "Minister of Magic,"Edinburgh Student Newspaper, 4 March 2008: 15.

books together, and I would wager a guess that neither does she as an author. Because of this, I will rarely attach J.K. Rowling's name to an idea. I will do so only in cases when I feel reasonably certain that the idea was consciously intended.

But does the fact that J.K. Rowling may not have set out to write fiction based on Christian principles undermine the integrity of this book? I don't think so, because any book is more meaningful than the sum of its author's intent; just as we can't know all the depths of our motivations, goals, and actions, neither can a writer, for whom characters are as real as actual people. It's like when a person goes to a psychologist for a neurosis they don't understand. The therapist can help them discover reasons for their unhealthy behaviors that have been there all along, but the person hasn't been able to notice it. The same goes for a novel. Just like a human being, it has many, many layers.

Now, just because we as readers can't know an author's intent doesn't mean that anything goes. Conjectures about the deeper meaning of a work have to seem reasonable given the boundaries of the story. This makes it unlikely that anyone could convincingly argue that Goyle saved the wizarding world, for instance. So within reason, I will be making arguments about how theological ideas play out in the series. We as readers may never know for sure if these were part of Rowling's scheme for the books, but as Dumbledore said to his protégé, "Of course it's happening in your head, Harry, but why on earth should that mean that it is not real?" (*DH*, 273).

CHAPTER 2:

Why the Dark Arts

The Problem of Evil

Looking evil in the eye

M Y STUDENTS AND I begin each semester with one of the most compelling human mysteries: evil. Every flavor cupcakes in hand—my real life equivalent of Bertie Bott's infamous jelly beans—the members of our seminar sit around the discussion table, look one another in the eye, and debate the nature and purpose of evil. We talk about what it means for Rowling's characters, what it means for Christians, and implicitly, what it means for them.

I begin by telling them that one of the most enduring and contentious topics in Christianity is the problem of evil, which asks how evil could exist given the presence of an all-knowing, all-good, and all-powerful God. After all, if God is all-good, then God would not want evil to exist; if God is all-powerful, then God should have the ability to prevent it, and if God is all-knowing, then God should recognize the harm evil does to creation. For many people, this tension between evil and the Christian God is the greatest challenge to their faith, while for others it is their greatest consolation. It is why some embrace Christianity and others turn away from it, why some find strength and others emptiness.

Christianity has no easy answer for why God and evil co-exist. But over its two thousand year existence, some of the greatest theologians have formulated theodicies—reasons why God would allow evil—to explain this phenomenon. The *Harry Potter* series is also interested in what causes evil and why it remains a powerful human force. In fact, Rowling told NBC's "Today" show that she wanted to do justice to evil's complexity. She said, "If you're writing about evil you genuinely have a responsibility to show what that means and that's why I'm writing [the books] the way I'm writing them."[6]

We're going to spend extensive time in this chapter understanding what Christianity and Rowling's books have to say about evil. In what follows, we will contrast two perspectives on theodicy called the free will defense and the soul-making theodicy. We will then use these frameworks to discuss how the *Harry Potter* books conceive the nature and purpose of evil.

Augustine and the Free Will Defense

Augustine of Hippo lived in present day Algeria during the late fourth and early fifth centuries and though he was the son of a Christian mother, Monica, he did not convert to Christianity until mid-life. He is one of the most formative thinkers in the Christian tradition, and his writings continue to influence the way many understand their faith and relationship to God.

In writing about the problem of evil, Augustine was trying to avoid blaming God or human nature for evil's origination. Here's why: Christians believe that God is all-good. They also believe that creation was made good. They subscribe to this view for two reasons: first, Genesis 1:27 says that humans are made "in the image" of God, so if God is all-good, then humans must be, by nature, good as well. Second, Genesis 1:31 says that God saw that creation was "very good," so by nature, creation is not evil. But if God is not to blame for evil and neither is something inherent in creation, then what is?

6   Associated Press, "Harry Potter author defends her work," 14 October 1999, 15 July 2009 <http://www.accio-quote.org/articles/1999/1099-ap.html>.

Augustine concluded that evil originated because humans abused their freedom; hence, his theodicy is called the free will defense. Augustine said the initial abuse occurred in the Garden of Eden, when Satan tempted Adam and Eve to eat the apple from a tree God explicitly told them to avoid. This bad choice predisposed humans to making subsequent choices that resulted in evil, causing a chronic and universal condition known as original sin. In this state, people are prone to exercise their free will inappropriately. To give a contemporary example, imagine that Joe Sixpack knows the dangers of alcohol, and he also knows that driving and drink shouldn't mix, but he hates wasting money on cabs, and he's wired to crave hard liquor. One night, he consumes five shots of whiskey and then drives home, causing a car accident that kills all passengers in the other vehicle because of his impaired judgment. In this case, Joe makes a conscious decision, knowing the risks taken could result in an evil, namely the loss of innocent lives. Joe Sixpack doesn't have to be a bad person to have made this error; he could still be a good father and love his wife. He might give more than his fair share to charities and take care of his elderly parents. Nonetheless, Joe abused his freedom when he drove home that night, and he ought to have known better.

Making use of the luggage analogy from the introduction, what stays in Augustine's suitcase and what gets removed? Let's deal with what Augustine chooses to pack first. Augustine is concerned with preserving the goodness of humans and God, so that stays in the suitcase. This conveniently avoids Augustine's concerns, namely blaming humans or God for being innately evil. By suggesting that the combination of human freedom and Satan's powers of temptation are to blame for evil's beginnings, both creation and God are implicitly off the hook. Yet that said, one is left wondering two things: first, why did God give humans the ability to choose evil, and second, why did God create Satan, a being who could lure humans towards evil?

Augustine would reply to the first objection by saying that humans have the ability to reason through their choices. To rob them of this ability would be to take away something that's essential to their nature, that defines them. Augustine's logic is reminiscent of contemporary critics of high school programs that force students to volunteer: it is not really volunteering, they argue, if one is forced to participate in it. Rather, a defining characteristic of volunteering is the fact that one *chooses* to participate in an unpaid activity. Likewise, if humans didn't have the ability to reason through a situation and choose a solution, they would be something other than human. We'll see that Rowling also puts a premium on choice a little later in the chapter.

In regards to why God would create Satan in the first place, Augustine suggested that God did not create an evil angel. Satan was a good angel who became evil when he sought to become like God and rebelled. Yet we have to wonder: why was Satan able to do such a thing? There are several possible reasons, but all of them are flawed:

Evil pre-existed God: This would give Satan the ability to rebel against God. But if God is supposed to be the creator in Christian thought, then how could evil exist prior to anything God made?

God created temptation: If God created temptation, then we have to wonder why—if temptation didn't exist, then Satan wouldn't have been able to rebel; likewise, human free will wouldn't be tempted because the option to be tempted wouldn't exist. As an example, let's say that Willy Wonka was offered a choice of eating a chocolate ice cream or mushy brussel sprouts. It seems more likely than not that Willy Wonka would choose the chocolate ice cream, even though it is high in fat and sugar and apt to make him prone to either a heart attack or diabetes. Now let's imagine that there was no such thing as chocolate ice cream and Willy was simply given mushy brussel sprouts. He wouldn't know what he was missing. From the same perspective, the fact that Satan could be tempted implies that God is responsible for evil by allowing temptation in the first place. That makes us wonder if Augustine's God is really all-good. Augustine never replies to this particular critique. This means that a solution that completely vindicates God's goodness as a creator seems to be discarded from the suitcase.

The final point I would like to make about Augustine has to do with the kind of evil Augustine seems to privilege. There are, within our world, many evils that are brought about by conscious choices: a man's coldblooded decision to murder his wife or a teenager's consistent bullying of another student. But there are also evils that one would be hard-pressed to argue arise from misuse of free will: a couple who dies in a fire because the battery in their smoke detector malfunctioned or a flood that destroys hundreds of homes by a river. While the free will defense might give some insight into those evils that are brought about by our choices, it doesn't seem to adequately explain the many forms of evil that are unintended, and in these cases, it encourages seeking blame where no blame is to be had.

Moreover, for our purposes, we are left wondering whether the free will defense is a way of explaining evil in Harry Potter's world. The series' emphasis on the theme of choice would point to some similarity of thought, but let's look at one other view of evil before answering specific questions about evil in the wizarding world.

Iranaeus, John Hick, and the Soul-Making Theodicy

If Augustine's theodicy seems to assume that all evils can be attributed to human choice, then Iranaeus and John Hick take a very different perspective. As we did with Augustine, let's begin by looking at the context of these writers, especially Iranaeus, to get a sense of what motivated their work. As we will see, their concerns were very different from Augustine, and as a result, so were their theodicies.

Iranaeus was a patristic writer, meaning that he is one of the earliest Christian thinkers (the word patristic comes from the Latin *patris*, which means father, so to be a patristic writer means to be a parent of Christian thought). Born in Smyrna, Turkey, in the second century, Iranaeus wrote on a variety of subjects, including theodicy, and his writing makes use of both the biblical tradition and elements of Greek philosophy. It was important to Iranaeus to blend these two ways of thinking together to show that a relationship between Greek thought and Christianity could exist.

Central to Iranaeus was an idea taken from the Greeks that humans are filled with potential and that during their lives, they have the opportunity to make that potential a reality. He interpreted this early verse in the Book of Genesis through this lens: "Then God said, 'Let us make humankind in our image, according to our likeness'" (Gen. 1:31). Iranaeus thought two words from this passage—image and likeness—were the key to understanding human development. At birth, humans are made in the image of God, and that is something they possess in fullness throughout life. In contrast, humans are not born into God's likeness. They come into the world in something of a childlike, immature state, and to reach their full potential, humans must grow into the likeness of God. As they develop and change, humans can become increasingly in God's likeness, and only once they are fully in both God's image and likeness have they reached the identity God intended for them.

Almost two thousand years later, contemporary philosopher of religion John Hick expanded Iranaeus's conception of image and likeness into a full-blown theodicy. He said that humans are born in the image of God, but through experiences of evil, they grow into the likeness. In other words, evil exists so that people can achieve divine likeness. To explain what he means, Hick uses the analogy of a parent with a child: all parents want their children to be comfortable and happy, to experience pleasure and avoid pain. Yet parents also realize that to expose their children only to pleasure, to spoil them, does not help them become mature adults; certain kinds of pain are good for them, such as the pain caused by inoculations or the discipline of a weekly allowance. Hick therefore reasons that some pain is good pain because it teaches important lessons that are necessary for children to grow into healthy, well-adjusted adults. Likewise for God-human relationships, Hick says. Just as a parent sometimes brings pain upon a child for the greater good of their development, so humans experience evil in order to grow into divine likeness, to reach their fullest potential. Hick thus surmises that evil exists for the purpose of soul-making, to bring the soul into the likeness of God. Hence, his theodicy is known as soul-making theodicy.

There is one great strength to this theodicy that is simultaneously its greatest weakness. Its strength lies in that it rings true with many human experiences of evil; many humans feel as if their experiences of evil do form them in powerful ways, that they learn valuable lessons from their sufferings, that pain has molded their character so that they are kinder, more compassionate and generous. People often believe that they learned something from their experiences that outweighs the power of the evil itself.

But for many others this is not the case. For some, experiences of evil are so horrific that it seems as if no good could possibly outweigh them. It is not hard to think of examples: systematic abuse, torture, war, sexualized violence, illness, or economic hardships immediately come to mind. These kinds of evils often leave victims so impaired that they are either incapable of learning anything from their experiences or, perhaps more disturbingly, these kinds of violations become a sign that there may not be anything to learn. It would seem in such instances that evil trumps any good that can come of it. To provide just one illustration, when Elie Wiesel wrote about of his experiences in a concentration camp during the Holocaust, he tells the story of Akiba Drumer, another member of the camp who was sentenced to death in the crematory. Wiesel remembers that prior to his death:

> He wandered among us, his eyes glazed, telling everyone of his weakness: 'I can't go on…It's all over….' It was impossible to raise his morale. He didn't listen to what we told him. He could only repeat that all was over for him, that he could no longer keep up the struggle, that he had no strength left, nor faith. Suddenly his eyes would become blank, nothing but two open wounds, two pits of terror.[7]

It may be that had Drumer lived long enough, he might have found some sort of knowledge or revelation that would have justified his extreme suffering, though this is not a given. The reality is that humans are frequently left speechless,

7 .   Elie Wiesel, *Night* (New York: Bantam Books, 1960).

hopeless, and without faith when faced with evils of such a magnitude, so that oftentimes evil does not lead to the kind of soul-making that Hick imagines, even when there is a lifetime of opportunities for it. In these cases, the effects of evil are devastating, not redemptive. The soul is not formed but crushed.

This, then, is the problem with Hick's theodicy, what he leaves out of the suitcase: evil may be used for the good of soul-making but it may also appear in such a way that any soul-making that does occur could not possibly outweigh the harm inflicted. In other words, while soul-making rings true to the experience of some, it rings false to the experience of others.

Lest we leave Hick and Iranaeus on a negative note, there is one last strength worth drawing out because of how it relates their theodicy to Augustine's. In Augustine's theodicy, evil arose because of the misuse of human freedom. This misuse is considered unfortunate because prior to eating the apple, Adam and Eve existed in their perfected state, but afterwards, humanity fell into its current, imperfect form. This event is thus known as the Fall in Augustinian discourse.

Soul-making theodicy does not view human development in that way. Hick and Iranaeus would say that Adam and Eve made the choice they did because they were not yet in the likeness of God; it was a natural and expected occurrence, and it was not necessarily a bad thing, as it is in the Augustinian framework. Hence, Adam and Eve's actions are not known as a Fall but rather a *felix culpa*, a lucky mistake or fortunate fall.

This distinction summarizes the biggest difference between the soul-making theodicy and the free will defense: in the former, evil is natural and beneficial for humans because it helps them learn and grow into the fullness of their being. In the latter, it is exactly the opposite.

This distinction also affects how each model understands what it means to be human. In the free will defense, evil arises because humans consciously make bad choices, and they are punished for them as a result. There is an assumption here that humans are in a position to be penalized: they ought to know what is right and wrong, and so when they act unwisely, they can be punished.[8] Consider, for instance, a baby who spits up on her mother's new evening gown. The mother would be hard pressed to punish her infant because the infant was not in control of her digestive system. Now, let's say this mother's evening gown was ruined by her teenager shooting paint balls at her. In this instance, the mother would likely punish her child, who ought to realize that behavior is inappropriate.

For Augustine, the ought-implies-can principle is a reality: humans are only punished for their poor choices because they ought to know better. They are more like the teenager than the infant. In the soul-making theodicy, this is not the case. Evil is seen as a natural byproduct of human freedom, a kind of hazard that comes with the game of free will. Humans cannot be punished because they are not really aware of what they are doing. Not being fully in the likeness of God yet, they are more like the infant than the teenager, and so they can't be held entirely responsible for the accidents that follow in their wake. It makes sense, then, that humans are not punished in this scenario—rather, evil is used for the purpose of soul-making. Hence, this framework seems to privilege those instances of evil that are unintended, like the couple mentioned above who are accidentally killed in a fire when the alarm fails to sound. That said, what this theodicy fails to capture are those instances of evil that are purposefully perpetrated and consciously carried out.

One may well argue that the free will defense takes a very different perspective than the soul-making theodicy does. Where the soul-making theodicy says that evil leads humans towards perfection, the free will defense argues that evil is an unfortunate mishap that pulled humans away from it. Whereas the soul-making theodicy exonerates humans in situations of evil, the free will defense holds them responsible. How this dichotomy will play out in Rowling's writings, we shall now see.

---

8   This idea is often attributed to the Enlightenment philosopher Immanuel Kant, and it is known in philosophical discourse as the ought-implies-can principle.

Theodicy in the *Harry Potter* series

If Rowling deals with any theological topic explicitly in her series, it is the problem of evil—from the first book of the series, characters navigate the waters of evil, trying to understand why it happens and how to respond to it. In fact, the whole series is framed by one overarching evil that influences every aspect of the books: the death of Harry's parents. Throughout the series, we see Harry figuring out the significance of his parents' martyrdom and what it means for him and the wizarding world. This evil motivates the entire series, and it isn't difficult to see that everything from Harry's personal development to the battle in book seven relates to this event.

Given that evil is so important to understanding the series, does Rowling understand evil from a perspective that resonates with Christianity's? Does she view its purpose through the lens of the free will defense or the soul-making theodicy, or is she working in a different system entirely?

Because of the series' emphasis on choice, we might expect to see free-will theodicy finding prominence, so let's start by seeing whether that's the case. We'll begin with Dumbledore. The reader learns in the seventh book that Dumbledore's ambition led, indirectly at least, to the murder of his disabled sister Ariana. When Dumbledore came home to care for his younger sibling after the death of his mother Kendra, he was distracted by the arrival of Grindelwald. Together the two concocted a plan to bring the wizarding world to power by overthrowing the rule of Muggles. Dumbledore neglected his duty to his family by privileging his friendship with Grindelwald, thereby causing his younger brother Aberforth to intervene and remind him to exchange pride and ambition for responsibility. A fight broke out between Grindelwald, Dumbledore, and Aberforth, and in the ensuing wandfire, Ariana was killed.

Reflecting on these events from his past, Dumbledore seems well-aware of how his choices were motivated by selfishness and greed: he desired to be great, famous, immortal, and he hoped that great power for the wizarding world would mean that he would have less responsibility for Ariana. After her death, Dumbledore realized the error in his ways. He said, "I was left to bury my sister, and learn to live with my guilt and my terrible grief, the price of my shame" (*DH*, 717).

The reader sees how responsible Dumbledore feels for the evils he inflicted not only in the above-mentioned passage, which takes place at King's Cross Station in book seven, but also at the end of *Half-Blood Prince*, when he drinks poison from the cup in the cave. Forced to recall the role he played in his sister's death, he cries out, "It's all my fault, all my fault... Please make it stop, I know I did wrong, oh please make it stop and I'll never, never again..." (*HBP*, 572). We as readers feel Dumbledore's anguish in that moment and see that he not only takes accountability for his choices but that he has suffered for his wrongdoings.

We see also see an emphasis upon choice when we consider Harry and Voldemort's development. In their early years, the protagonist and villain have remarkably similar upbringings. Both are raised as orphans in inhospitable environments—Harry with the Dursleys and Voldemort in the orphanage. Both grow up unaware of the wizarding world or their place in it, and both have the capacity to perpetrate evils—Voldemort because of his ambition and Harry because of his tendency for isolation and jealousy. In many ways, they are given the same lot in life, and yet their trajectories could not be more different.

Rowling seems to emphasize over and over again that choice is what shapes the paths Harry and Voldemort take. Nowhere is this more explicit than at the end of *Chamber of Secrets*, when Harry worries about his relationship to evil, confessing to Dumbledore that he suspects there is a core of evil inside him, a core that should have committed him to Slytherin House. Dumbledore replies:

> "Listen to me, Harry. You happen to have many qualities Salazar Slytherin prized in his hand-picked students. His own very rare gift, Parseltongue—resourcefulness—determination—a certain disregard

for rules," he added, his mustache quivering again. "Yet the Sorting Hat placed you in Gryffindor. You know why that was. Think."

"It only put me in Gryffindor," said Harry in a defeated voice, "because I asked not to go in Slytherin...."

"*Exactly*," said Dumbledore, beaming once more. "Which makes you very *different* from Tom Riddle. It is our choices, Harry, that show what we truly are, far more than our abilities" (*CS*, 333).

This selection demonstrates the extent to which choice determines Harry and Voldemort's relationship to evil—for Voldemort, evils exist because he chose to inflict them; likewise, Harry's commitment to shunning evil, even to the point of his own death, is a choice for which he is rewarded.

As a final example of free-will theodicy at work in the series, let's turn to Ron Weasley. Throughout the series Ron is plagued by feelings of insecurity that play out in the evils he perpetrates: dating Lavender Brown to make himself feel better about not having kissed anyone or abandoning Harry and Hermione during their search for Horcruxes. The reader recognizes that Ron's evils are perpetrated less out of malice than out of fear that he is unworthy or unlovable. Even the Horcrux necklace picks up on that, weakening Ron in all the areas in which he is least confident (*DH* 307). But just because his motives are clear doesn't mean his actions aren't evil. They have serious consequences for Harry and Hermione: his absence leaves them despondent, lonely, frustrated, heartbroken, and somewhat hopeless.

When Ron finally locates his friend, Harry is in the throes of death, being strangled by the Horcrux around his neck. Ron rescues him and then, facing the Horcrux that led him to abandon his friends, he confronts those inner demons that fueled his insecurities. The Horcrux taunts him:

> "*Least loved, always, by the mother who craved a daughter...Least loved, now, by the girl who prefers your*

friend…Second best, always, eternally overshadowed…
Who could look at you, who would ever look at you,
beside Harry Potter? What have you ever done,
compared with the Chosen One? What are you,
compared with the Boy Who Lived?" (DH 375-6).

Ron responds by piercing the Horcrux, killing not only a piece of Voldemort's soul but also those voices of temptation that held sway for so many years.

Interestingly, the Horcrux's influence on Ron is reminiscent of another powerful substance we talked about earlier in this chapter. Recall the illustration of the free will theodicy mentioned above, where we discussed the influence alcohol had over Joe Sixpack. He had a chemical weakness for liquor, which is what made him an alcoholic; when he drank, it impaired his judgment and led to the accident. We could set up an analogy with Ron and the Horcrux: his insecurities are like Joe's alcoholism, and the Horcrux's influence is like the influence of the liquor itself. It was as hard for Ron to resist the Horcrux as it was for Joe to resist drinking, but because both gave into their weaknesses, evils occurred. Likewise, only when Ron ceased to let the Horcrux overpower him was he able to overcome the insecurities that let it hold sway in the first place. In this way, we might say that there are hints of the soul-making theodicy in Ron's story—his soul is certainly made from the evils he experiences, though they are certainly chosen willfully.

This brings us to soul-making. Are other examples of this theodicy present in the books? Consider Draco Malfoy, whose evils pervade the series, ranging from the petty pranks he plays upon Harry—recall the "Potter Stinks" buttons—to his attempted murder of Dumbledore. He is not shy with his insults, taunting everyone from Neville Longbottom to his right-hand men Crabbe and Goyle; he has no scruples about pushing others aside so that he can get ahead, and he introduces Harry to one of the few truly derogatory words in the wizarding world: Mudblood.

Rowling makes no secret of Malfoy's allegiances, allowing her character to clearly voice them in the first conversation Harry has with him in Diagon Alley, when the two discuss the issue of blood lineage: "I really don't think they should let the other sort in, do you?" Draco says. "They're just not the same, they've never been brought up to know our ways. Some of them have never even heard of Hogwarts until they get the letter, imagine. I think they should keep it in the old wizarding families. What's your surname, anyway?" (*SS*, 78).

Yet from the time that we as readers meet Draco, it is hard to hold him accountable for his actions because Rowling repeatedly highlights that he's a product of his upbringing, promoting the exclusionary, bigoted priorities of his parents. No one can compete with their influence. While other characters series rally around Dumbledore's values of love and acceptance, Draco finds himself drawn in by his father's power, a power in which he is invested because it provides him security and privilege. Nowhere is this more clearly stated than in *Chamber of Secrets* just after Dumbledore's expulsion from the school. Bragging in potions class, Draco says, "'I always thought Father might be the one who got rid of Dumbledore,' he said, not troubling to keep his voice down. 'I told you he thinks Dumbledore's the worst headmaster the school's ever had'" (*CS*, 266-7).

Draco may become the most strident advocate within Hogwarts for the warped values of the Death Eaters, but it is often hard to blame him. Instead of judgment, we as readers feel sympathy for a boy who is clearly the product of his upbringing, an upbringing that promoted coercion rather than choice. Nowhere is this more prominent than at the end of book six, when Draco, standing with a wand pointed at the defenseless Dumbledore, struggles with the job that Voldemort set for him. Dumbledore tries to convince him to abandon the mission, and in this moment, the reader sees how little autonomy Draco perceives himself as having. "I can help you, Draco," Dumbledore says to his attacker. "'No you can't,' said Malfoy, his wand shaking very badly indeed. 'Nobody can. He told me to do it or he'll kill me. I've got no choice'" (*HP*, 591).

I've got no choice, Draco says. This encapsulates his relationship to evil—he perpetrates crimes because too much is invested with his parents for him entertain other options.

His family's world provides superiority and comfort whereas Dumbledore's ideals may be noble, but for Draco, they offer uncertainty and would require him to abandon all that the Malfoys raised him to believe. In this way, it is easy for us to see that Draco wasn't really born a bigot; he was raised to be that way. Could we really expect a child with Lucius as a father and Bellatrix as an aunt to turn out any differently?

As the song from *South Pacific* goes, "You've got to be taught to hate and fear. You've got to be taught from year to year....You've got to be taught before it's too late, before you are six or seven or eight, to hate all the people your relatives hate, you've got to be carefully taught!"[9] Draco is taught so well that when the time comes for him to choose between what is right and what is easy—to use Dumbledore's language—he doesn't have the tools to make that decision (*GF*, 724). As a result, he comes off as pitiable more than punishable. Just as Hick and Iranaeus might postulate, Draco is a child who has been misguided and manipulated throughout his young life, and so his evils occur more often than not because he is incapable of other alternatives. So he is right to say, in that moment when his wand is pointed at Dumbledore, that he doesn't have a choice. The tragedy is that he does have a choice, but he is unable to realize it.

But if Draco is imaged as Hick and Iranaeus suggest, if he is indeed a creature who is full of potential, then is that potential ever fulfilled or is Malfoy permanently damaged by the way in which his potential has been misused? Put differently, is his soul ever made? Looking to the end of book seven and the reader's last image of Draco, it would seem as if his soul is only half made, shall we say. There is something about Rowling's last portrayal of this character that is empty, sad. He is described as a man with a prematurely receding hairline and a kind of repressed demeanor, which leaves the reader feeling as if he isn't flourishing in the way Ron, Harry, and Hermione are—

---

9   Original Broadway cast, "You've Got To Be Carefully Taught," *South Pacific*, by Richard Rogers and Oscar Hammerstein II, Sony, 1949. I am indebted to my former student, Rachel Miller-Ziegler, for relating the elements of discrimination in this song to those in Harry's world.

while they chat happily amongst each other, Draco stands apart from them, silent, voiceless (*DH*, 755-6). We will never know what he is thinking, whether he has been able to overcome those influences that caused him to perpetrate prior evils. One might assume, since he is not in Azkaban, that he has kept his tendencies at bay, either because his priorities have changed or because he has the good sense not to make them known in a post-war wizarding world that does not privilege them. Regardless, the difference between the vibrancy of the other characters and Draco is striking, and he seems to bear within him a heaviness, a darkness that the other characters lack. In this way, he may exemplify one of the shortcomings of the soul-making theodicy by showing that some evils do not make the soul; rather, these evils have a power so pervasive that they cannot be overcome.

Draco Malfoy is one example of partial soul-making at work in the series, but let's look at two other characters who bring this theodicy to its fulfillment. First, we will think about Harry himself. Earlier in this chapter we discussed how Harry and Voldemort exemplified the free will defense, but Harry also experiences evils that form his soul. From the start of Harry's orphanhood, Dumbledore tries to shape the young boy into the person he will need to be to defeat the Dark Lord. He places him with the Dursleys and not a wizarding family because he didn't want him to grow up conceited by his own fame. He also gives Harry guidance when he encounters evil so that instead of being blistered by it, those experiences provide the basis for a pure and loving soul.

Consider the death of Harry's parents as an evil. Harry himself may not see the way in which his soul has been formed by their martyrdom, but Dumbledore encourages him to read the loss through that lens. He explains to Harry in book six that their death is the force that protects his soul from perpetrating the kind of evils that appealed to Voldemort. As Dumbledore explains to Harry:

> "You have never been seduced by the Dark Arts, never, even for a second, shown the slightest desire to become

one of Voldemort's followers!"

"Of course I haven't!" said Harry indignantly. "He killed my mum and dad!"

"You are protected, in short, by your ability to love!" said Dumbledore loudly. "The only protection that can possibly work against the lure of power like Voldemort's! In spite of all the temptation you have endured, all the suffering, you remain pure of heart, just as pure as you were at the age of eleven, when you stared into a mirror that reflected your heart's desire, and it showed you only the way to thwart Lord Voldemort, and not immortality or riches" (*HBP*, 511).

Though no one would wish the death of one's parents as a means to teach love, it is nonetheless a fact for Harry that this horrific loss became something that shaped him in powerful and beautiful ways, preventing him from developing the kind of misplaced priorities that define the Dark Lord. In other words, the loss of his parents shaped his soul.

We might look at the role Sirius's death played in Harry's development as well. Harry rails at Dumbledore following the loss of his godfather with an honesty that touches the core of the human experience of grief. The loss of a friend or family member is painful precisely because we loved them, and because the grief is so uncomfortable, it's natural to try to avoid it. But Dumbledore realizes that it is impossible to live healthily or to love when one avoids feeling. He tells Harry:

"There is no shame in what you are feeling, Harry," said Dumbledore's voice. "On the contrary…the fact that you can feel pain like this is your greatest strength."

Harry felt the white-hot anger lick his insides, blazing in the terrible emptiness, filling him with the desire to hurt Dumbledore for his calmness and his empty words.

"My greatest strength, is it?" said Harry, his voice shaking as he stared out at the Quidditch stadium, no longer seeing it. "You haven't got a clue...You don't know..."

"What don't I know?" asked Dumbledore calmly.

It was too much. Harry turned around, shaking with rage.

"I don't want to talk about how I feel, all right?"

"Harry, suffering like this proves you are still a man! This pain is part of being human—"

"THEN—I—DON'T—WANT—TO—BE—HUMAN!" Harry roared (*OP* 823-4).

As this episode progresses, Dumbledore responds calmly to Harry, giving him the space to vocalize his grief all the while imparting the information he needs to understand why Sirius died and how his death fits into the narrative of the war between good and evil in Harry's world. He tells Harry here, as he does in book six, that the evil he experienced is also that which protects his purity of heart.

Late in book seven, it is precisely that purity which allows Harry to offer his life for the wizarding world. In that moment, we see the fulfillment of his soul-making process. Harry has reached the likeness of God—to use the biblical term—and that moment becomes the culmination of years of learning to love well, even when the consequences of loving were painful. We will be spending much more time on Harry's death in the chapter on sacrifice, but insofar as his death relates to evil, let us say for now that the love with which he offered his life shows that his soul has indeed been made.

And now, let us turn to Dumbledore. Recall that we discussed Dumbledore in the section on free will defense, and even though choices were so integral to his development, I would argue that he had a soul shaped both by the evil he chose and that which was chosen by those around him. For instance, while Rowling underscores Dumbledore's liability, she also emphasizes that he learned from his mistakes. Dumbledore spent his entire life advocating for the rights of underprivileged Squibs, Muggles, and Mudbloods after the death of Ariana, thereby showing that he recognized his errors and tried to atone for them. So while Dumbledore perpetrated evils in a way that resonates with the free will defense, he handled the aftermath of his offenses in a way that was more analogous to the soul-making theodicy. Few characters in the books have souls as full of love as wisdom as Dumbledore's; few are as self-actualized or self-giving. Dumbledore, like Harry, becomes a fulfilled person both because of the evils he perpetrates and the ones that make his soul.

What this demonstrates is that Harry and Dumbledore's characters are a unique amalgam of Augustine, Iranaeus, and Hick that mirrors the series overall. Hence, we might say that the series presents both the free will defense and the soul-making theodicy side by side. This is a clever move. As explained above, both of these theodicies have their strengths and their limitations, but Rowling eliminates the problems that arise when one chooses one over the other by presenting them together. Alongside one another, they illustrate a more comprehensive picture of evil than they do alone.

Interestingly, Rowling herself has touched upon the ways in which both theodicies appear in the books, though she doesn't use theological language to do so. In an interview with *The Associated Press*, she said, "I think they're very moral books. The children…have to make their own choices. I see all three of them as innately good people," Rowling said. "I see children as innately good unless they've been very damaged. That's where I'm coming from."[10]

Rowling does two things in this quotation: she emphasizes the importance of choice while also recognizing that situational influences can be overpowering. In this way, she drives home that people respond differently to evil given their

10   Associated Press, "Harry Potter author defends her work," 14 October 1999, 15 July 2009 <http://www.accio-quote.org/articles/1999/1099-ap.html>.

background and abilities. Draco may simply be too "damaged" to be able understand that he always has a choice to do good over evil; for characters like Dumbledore, that is not the case. Characters also have the opportunity to learn from the evils they perpetrate, and sometimes, as with Ron, that learning is so profound that it heals their deepest inadequacies.

What then can we conclude about the *Harry Potter* series and its depiction of evil? While it resonates with Christianity's take on evil, it avoids the doctrinaire. The books are unique in that they present two theodicies and show how each reinforces the other using a variety of characters and situations. Does this mean the books align with a Christian worldview? Most certainly. Do they present any ideas about evil that directly contradict Christianity? None that this writer can see.

Moving Beyond Evil

By the end of our first class together, the every flavor cupcakes were gone, and some students had experienced their own evils in the form of Tabasco sauce, ketchup, or curry fillings! But what I also saw—in addition to some green faces—was passion and excitement. At moments, virtually every student had his or her hand raised to make a comment at the same time, something unheard of in most classrooms. Their enthusiasm testified that regardless of one's faith, the question of why evil exists and the role it plays in life is one of the most profound questions any human asks. What the *Harry Potter* series suggests is that there is no one answer to this question but a variety of truths—that evil can arise from choice or victimization, that it devastates as easily as it strengthens.

Whether or not my students agree with this personally is something they must grapple with outside the classroom, as they encounter personal evils in whatever form they may take. Of course, I want none of them to suffer pain or grief, but I also know it is one of the costs we pay to be alive. Yet I hope that by the end of our time together, they will have a new way to ask the question, "Why evil?" And perhaps that may make their burden just a little bit lighter.

Questions for Your Reflection

1)	What other characters in the Harry Potter series have experiences of evil? How does either the free-will theodicy or the soul-making theodicy frame this character's experience? For instance, reflect on Remus Lupin, Glideroy Lockhart, and Kreacher.

2)	What events in the wizarding world caused moments of evil that were started by some, but felt by all? How do we understand theodicy in these cases? Think about the rise of Grindewald, Voldemort, and the lies of the *Daily Prophet*.

3)	How have you dealt with evil in your own life? Did you or someone else choose evil or was it brought upon you? How has that shaped your experience? Is it possible to see the free-will theodicy and soul-making theodicy acting together in your life as Rowling weaves it together in the series?

4)	In Ron's life, evil seems to originate from lies directed at his confidence. Where else does evil begin in certain Harry Potter characters? Think about Peter Pettigrew, Horace Slughorn, and Bellatrix Lestrange.

CHAPTER 3

Choosing what is Right Instead of Easy

Sin

Defining Sin

B Y THE SECOND WEEK of the term, I began to see the weight of the semester bearing down. Vacation was clearly over: problem sets were due; snowstorms which appeared charming caused dorm rooms to be covered by a thin layer of sand and salt. Everyone, including myself, felt permanently cold to the core, regardless of being outdoors or in, and no one wanted to do anything but stay in bed, under the covers and preferably next to a heater.

In our seminar, I saw that heaviness on the faces of my students, and not just because of the weather. Unlike evil, which was a naturally provocative topic, talking about sin made them uneasy. Many found it uncomfortable to think that humans are sinners by nature. This is an interesting phenomenon because historically, Christians felt that the universality of sin was a source of comfort. Instead of feeling embarrassed or guilty, people knew that sin was a given. But over time, many lost that sense of succor and instead began viewing sin as something that could be avoided as opposed to something permanent, like cellulite or a cowlick. Because of that, the idea that people were sinners yielded a sense of shame instead of solace.

So one of the most important things I did in that class was to make sure my students understood what sin is and also what it's not. And the first step needed is to explain that sin and evil are not the same thing. As we saw in the last chapter, evil involves an act of some sort that yields negative consequences. The decision to kill one's nasty boss would be an evil; a flood that destroys a coastal village would also be an evil. Evils are incidents that vary in magnitude from the unpleasant to the absolutely horrific, from conscious choices to accidents, from psychological struggles to physical illnesses, and from human acts to natural occurrences. But whatever form they take, they are occurrences of some sort.

In contrast, sin is defined not as an event but as an overall orientation or disposition towards God that affects the entire person, not just their body or soul. (As an aside, remember this part about how sin affects the entire person. It will be important when we talk about Apollinaris in the Christology chapter.) When a person is not in proper relationship to God, he or she is said to be in a state of sin. As a result, sin is often defined as a turning away from God that results in warped values, desires, hopes, motives, and actions. The last of these—actions—shows that there is some overlap between sin and evil because a choice made when one is in a sinful state can result in an evil. For instance, Voldemort's inability to engage in right relationships causes him to perpetrate great evils in the wizarding world.

Another way of thinking about this is to say that all sins are evil, but not all evils are sins. Sinful thoughts and actions have an element of evil to them, but it would be hard to suggest that a flood is a sin because floods are not the work of human hands or misplaced attitudes. Now, if the flood were a result of global warming caused by humanity's poor environmental practices, then that would be a different story!

Christians often have more nuanced understandings of sin, and they that believe sin takes many guises. So we're going to start this chapter by engaging two conceptions of sin: the classical understanding of sin forwarded by Augustine and contemporary theologian Serene Jones's understanding of sin as unfaithfulness. The second part of the chapter will make use of these theories in order to discuss the presence of sin in the *Harry Potter* series.

Augustine and the Classic Conception of Sin:

For a majority of Christian history, there has been a dominant understanding of sin and its power. In this conception, Adam and Eve were free from sin in the Garden of Eden, but then they refused to recognize their proper place as humans and desired to be like God. This happened when the serpent lured them into eating from the forbidden tree saying, "God knows that when you eat of it [the tree] your eyes will be opened and you will be like God, knowing good and evil" (Gen. 3:5). Adam and Eve therefore ate of the tree because they desired to be wise like the Divine. Put differently, they were not satisfied with who they were created to be, which is why this first sin is said to be one of pride and disobedience.

Christian tradition says that Adam and Eve found themselves in a permanent state of sin because of their inappropriate desire. It also says that God punished them by forcing them out of the Garden and by making them experience pain and hardship. To make the situation worse, all future humans inherited Adam and Eve's punishment, causing them to be predisposed to inappropriate values and actions, just like the inappropriate values and actions of their forebears. The end result is that humans have to work harder than they should to attain the right values, beliefs, and priorities, but had Adam and Eve not sinned, this would not be the case. This idea that sin can be passed along from generation to generation and is present at birth is known as original sin.

As you can see, this understanding of sin ties in nicely with Augustine's view of evil. For Augustine, evil originated because of Adam and Eve's misplaced choices, for which they were punished because they should have known better. This state of sin is then passed from generation to generation as a punishment for Adam and Eve's first transgression. So one might say that in this framework Adam and Eve were responsible for their actions and had to bear the consequences, consequences that affected all future generations of humanity.

A Contemporary Image of Sin

For a variety of reasons, contemporary theologians are offering new interpretations of the traditional Christian conception of sin. Some do not like the way this framework understands original sin, finding it hard to believe that a baby is born in a state of sin. Others have trouble with the negative view of sexuality implicit in this framework because the traditional reasoning is that sin has to be transferred some way, and so if babies are sinful, then the process that makes them is sinful as well. Others feel that this view of sin is too narrow, focusing only on individual sins and sins of pride. These are just a few of the reasons why theologians have reworked what sin is and what it looks like. Their hope is to develop theologies that express the deep truth of what sin is and to develop a vocabulary for sin that makes this ancient concept resonate with modern audiences.

Contemporary theologian Serene Jones is one of those thinkers. Jones comes from the Reformed Christian tradition and her work is frequently feminist in orientation. She is an ordained minister and also the first female president of Union Theological Seminary in New York City. I am drawing upon her work here both because of her expansive understanding of sin and because of the way in which her conception of sin is an excellent example of the kind of thinking done by other modern theologians.

Jones writes that she was motivated to reframe the discussion of sin because of fallout from the classical conception. She writes that,

> Sin, however, has been interpreted in many ways in the Christian tradition, not all of them good. Talk of sin has been the occasion for debilitating shame or for the social marginalization of whole groups of people, often with devastating results. In cases like this, sin-talk functions as a weapon that harms or divides people. Such ways of talking about sin, indeed, are so common that my students find it hard to believe that understanding ourselves as sinners could have the long-term positive effects of deepening our faith, making us kinder and more open to others, less arrogant and un-self-critical,

and more realistic about life and its possibilities. But such goals lie at the heart of a classical Christian account of sin.[11]

Jones uses a different vocabulary to explain what sin is and how it affects us in order to rework such distortions. Instead of imaging sin as pride, Jones suggests that sin is fundamentally a state of unfaithfulness. In a state of unfaithfulness, humans live against God's will, meaning that they do not live into the wholeness or fullness that God intended for them at the time of Adam and Eve's creation.

But what does this fullness look like? Jones writes that there are seven characteristics of what it means to be human, which she calls the seven features of our creatureliness. They are:

1. Humans exist only because God called them into being.
2. God believes humanity is inherently good.
3. Humans are meant to be diverse: they are different from God and different from each other.
4. God wants a relationship with humans.
5. Humans are embodied and are also bound by time.
6. Humans are free creatures.
7. God wants humans to live healthy, fulfilling lives, and God makes a covenant with them to this end. In this covenant, God gives humans directions about how to flourish through the witness of the Bible, as well as personal and cultural experience. God also promises not to abandon them.[12] For as God says in the Book of Leviticus, "I will walk among you, and will be your God, and you shall be my people" (26:12). It is up to humans to choose whether to live in this covenant, because as free people, humans have a choice to live by the covenant or disregard it; God will not coerce people.[12]

---

11   Serene Jones, "Human Beings as Creatures of God," *Essentials of Christian Theology*, ed. William C. Placher (Louisville: Westminster John Knox Press, 2003) 148.

12   *Ibid.* 143-6.

When humans agree to live by this covenant, they live in faithfulness to God, but when they choose differently, they enter into a state of unfaithfulness, or sin.[13] Unfaithfulness takes seven forms that correspond to the seven characteristics of our creatureliness. These are:

1. **Pride as sin:** In this sin, humans deny that they are God's created beings and instead think of themselves as gods. They think that they can control their destinies, create themselves, or dominate others. They refuse to recognize that they are dependent upon God.

2. **Misunderstanding the goodness of creation as sin:** Humans believe that they are basically bad, or they forget that they are God's beloved creation and instead believe that there is something fundamentally wrong with themselves. This sin can take many forms: humans might believe that their bodies or minds are bad or they might believe that some lives are more valuable than others.

3. **Sameness as sin:** Humans forget that diversity is good and that they are meant to be distinct from God and each other. Instead, they try to make all people the same and commit idolatry by idolizing one way of living over all others. This sin can also take the form of enmeshment.

4. **Isolation as sin:** In this form of sin, humans do not engage in a relationship with God or with others. This sin is psychologically contagious in a way: when humans live in an environment where other people besides themselves are in imperfect relationships, they experience the fallout of those relationships even if they do not participate in them. For instance, a child whose parents are in an abusive relationship may experience a host of difficulties even though no abuse was personally inflicted upon them.

5. **Misunderstanding our nature as sin:** Here humans disregard the way in which they are social beings who exist in a certain time and place. Forms of this sin add greater depth to other forms already discussed because when people refuse to acknowledge what it means to be

13   *Ibid*, 149.

human, they are apt to commit sins like those of pride or sameness, to give just two examples.

6. **Misuse of freedom as sin:** Humans recognize that they have the freedom to choose not to sin, and yet they cannot help but sin. With so much sin around them, it becomes ingrained in them, and they cease to believe that certain sins are actually wrong. As an example, consider a song you heard on the radio that you initially didn't like. Unfortunately, it's a top ten hit and is played over and over again on your favorite station. One day you find yourself listening to the song and actually think, "You know, this isn't so bad." You begin to sing along when it comes on-air, and you may even go out and purchase the song for yourself. Now, you wouldn't have been exposed to the song had the disc jockey not played it repeatedly, and the disc jockey might not have played it so often if he wasn't getting a bonus from the record company. Of course, listening to awful music is not technically a sin, but it shows how repeated exposure to anything—even if it's something we don't like—can sway us to believe that it's desirable. This means that people have a tendency to choose sinful actions or beliefs because that is what surrounds them. This is Jones's equivalent of original sin, her explanation of why sin is experienced by all and passed from generation to generation. Note how she relies less on biology to explain sin's transmission and more on social structures.

7. **Misusing the covenant as sin:** People are supposed to live in relationship to God but sin by breaking the laws of the covenant. Humans also sin when we take the law too seriously, interpreting the letter of the law at the expense of its true spirit.[14]

Jones writes that human sin makes God angry, but she is careful to acknowledge that this wrath isn't because God is angry with humans. Rather, God is angry at sin and the way sin keeps people from living healthy,

14   *Ibid.* 150-154.

vibrant lives. This means that divine wrath is not a symbol of hatred but a symbol of God's deep and abiding love, a symbol of the pain God experiences when we are hurting.[15]

Finally, Jones is careful to show that sin can be committed not only by individuals but also by groups of people. For instance, a business might exploit laborers in order to make cheaper products; when people purchase those products, they contribute to the perpetuation of such inhumane practices. This is an example of social or corporate sin because it is sin committed by a whole group. Some members of the group may be more aware of the sin than others—the CEO of the company, who knows of the unfair labor practices, likely is more informed than the average consumer. Yet the consumer still contributes to the problem by purchasing the product made by the company. This kind of sin is harder to recognize because often individuals are not fully aware that they are involved in the problem. Other times, individuals are aware but do not perceive the issue as problematic enough to warrant their attention. In this way, corporate sin may be even more insidious than individual sin.[16]

Sin in the *Harry Potter* series

Discussing sin in the series is perhaps one of the thornier issues we will tackle because Rowling never uses the language of sin in her books. So does that mean that there's nothing like sin in Harry's world? *Au contraire.* Characters in the series certainly have dispositions that Christianity would regard as sinful, and, as I will argue, the books perceive the attitudes of these characters in the same way that Christianity would: as imperfect states to be transcended.

Let's look at the classical conception of sin first: central features of this framework include a Fall and the role of temptation in bringing about sin. I would like to present one possibility for how the books portray these principles. We don't know much about the origins of wizards, where they came from or how they originated. Rather, the closest equivalent we have in *Harry Potter* to something like those early chapters of Genesis—

15   *Ibid.* 149.
16   *Ibid.* 152-3.

which document creation and the Fall—is the story the creation of Hogwarts by the four founders. We are told that Salazar Slytherin, Helga Hufflepuff, Rowena Ravenclaw, and Godric Gryffindor decided to form Hogwarts together during a time of persecution, and they hoped that by hiding the school in a secret location, they would be able to safely educate wizarding youth. Initially, each founder was allowed to choose its own members: Slytherin chose students who were most cunning; Hufflepuff chose those who worked hardest; Ravenclaw picked the ones who were most intelligent and Gryffindor, the bravest. Yet after awhile, Slytherin's standards for admission to Hogwarts deviated from the other founders: he wanted only pure-blooded wizards to be admitted to the school whereas the other three founders wanted to educate all wizards, regardless of their lineage. Discord arose amongst the four founders, and Slytherin left as a result.

Reading this story through a classical theological lens makes it seem as if Slytherin fell prey to the same kind of temptation as Adam and Eve: he was tempted by pride, by a desire to elevate wizards to a higher status—or at least what he perceived to be a higher status. This kind of arrogance led to animosity in the wizarding world, animosity that persisted for generations and led to the conflict between Harry and Voldemort. In this way, the story of the four founders might be a parallel to the story of the Fall in Christianity: sin originated through the temptation of one person, in this case Salazar Slytherin. Or to be really crafty with this interpretation, one could also say that Slytherin functions as the serpent in Genesis 3 because he, like the serpent, brings sin into a sinless world. This would mean that the sinful state of the wizarding world developed through Slytherin's temptation of others. Gives Slytherin House's snake mascot a whole new meaning, doesn't it?

While compelling, the one problem with this analogy is that within the classical vision, original sin is passed down through the generations at birth, biologically in some way. We see no evidence of this kind of transmission in the wizarding world. The most prominent sins—intolerance and the lack of community created by this intolerance—are perpetuated because they are popularized within certain circles, not because they are biologically based. (Keep these two sins in mind! We're going to return to them in the chapter on salvation.)

It would seem that the way in which sin is passed along is more like the misuse of freedom sin (#6) in Serene Jones's framework: discrimination against Mudbloods and the lack of community that this discrimination creates are the result of faulty relationships, in which pure-bloods believe they are superior. When other wizards are exposed enough to this mindset, they too begin to believe its truth.

Indeed, because Jones has such a comprehensive vision of sin, it is easier to locate parallels between the *Harry Potter* series' ideas about sin and Christianity's. Let's look at a few examples. First, the sin of pride. Several instances—besides the previous example concerning Slytherin—are particularly notable here. Take Nicolas Flamel, who found the elixir of eternal life in the *Sorcerer's Stone*. The Stone which Flamel created could be used to develop an elixir that extended the life of humans indefinitely, and yet, Rowling is clear that Flamel's work was not in the wizarding world's best interest because it made people like Voldemort believe that they could control their destinies, become their own gods, be their own creators. In other words, the way that Voldemort desired the Stone shows his disposition towards the sin of pride. We as readers see this most clearly when Dumbledore says to Harry at the end of the first book, "You know, the Stone was really not such a wonderful thing. As much money and life as you could want! The two things human beings would choose above all—the trouble is, humans do have a knack for choosing precisely those things that are worst for them" (SS, 297).

The second example of the sin of pride: Dumbledore's values during his early years. His desire to control the wizarding world and achieve the Deathly Hallows for his own immortality demonstrates how he desired to hold powers that are not for wizards, however great they may be. Dumbledore's history, like Nicolas Flamel's, shows the evils that are done when one is disposed to pride: in Dumbledore's case, his misplaced priorities encouraged Grindelwald's destructive mission and led to the death of his sister Ariana; in the case of Nicolas Flamel, creation of the Sorcerer's Stone led to the death of unicorns and Ron's injury in wizarding chess. In this way, we see the way in which the inappropriate values of Dumbledore and Flamel led to sinful actions and consequences.

The *Harry Potter* books also highlight the sin of isolation. The most prominent example of this: recall when Dumbledore says that Voldemort refused friendships from an early age, a mindset that prevented him from trusting or loving and, in turn, made him cold-blooded and murderous. But Voldemort is not the only character who tends towards isolation: Harry is like that as well. Especially in the later books, Harry often shies away from the support of his friends because he thinks it is preferable to go it alone. In the fifth book, he eschews Hermione's advice that they try to contact Sirius before rushing to the Ministry of Magic, and refusing to hear the reasonableness of her suggestion eventually results in Sirius's death. At the end of the sixth book, he tells Ron and Hermione that they should stay with their families rather than embark on the search for elusive Horcruxes, though they want to come and Harry might well have failed his mission had they not. In the seventh book, Harry tries to convince Dumbledore's Army not to fight with him, which again could have been disastrous had they agreed. In this last instance particularly, Harry seems to be unaware that others want to fight, that they too have a personal stake in Voldemort's defeat. Put differently, Harry has a sense that it's all about him, his mission, his prophecy, and his vengeance, and it's hard for him to see that others are invested as well: Neville because Voldemort tortured his parents, Ginny because she loves her future husband, or Hermione because hers will be the first name on the Mudblood death list. When Harry opts for the solitary instead of solidarity, he is acting in a prideful way that ignores the needs of others.

This tendency is something Dumbledore is concerned about and tries to combat throughout the series. For example, he makes sure that Harry tells Hermione and Ron about the prophecy at the beginning of *Half-Blood Prince* so that he doesn't carry that knowledge alone. He also leaves Hermione and Ron the Deluminator and *Tales of Beedle the Bard* as if to ensure that they participate in the search for Hallows and Horcruxes. So Dumbledore, like Christian theologians, recognizes the danger of going-it-alone and does his best to guide Harry toward a healthy life rooted in love and friendship.

As an aside, it is important to recognize that Harry's tendency towards isolation is different from the end of the books when Harry goes alone to his death. This distinction is rooted in Harry's motive. The act of walking to his death is undertaken not out of selfishness or convenience but rather out of a love for others that is at great cost to himself. His actions at the end of the novels actually point to the antithesis of pride— self-giving—but we're jumping ahead here. Stay tuned for the chapter on salvation when we'll return to that idea!

Harry's tendency towards isolation also affects other parts of his disposition, sometimes causing him to have an excessive sense of his own worth. Nicolas Wandinger, Christoph Drexler, and Teresa Peter discuss this issue in their article "Harry Potter and the Art of Theology I." They explain that at the beginning of *Order of the Phoenix*, Harry protects Dudley Dursley from the Dementors by producing a Patronus. After failing twice, he remembers his two friends Ron and Hermione and the happiness of that memory allows him to defend himself and protect his cousin. In this way, he forms the Patronus not alone, but through the help of his friends. However, when Harry feels rejected because he was not made prefect but Ron and Hermione were, he reinterprets the past. Wandinger, Drexler, and Peter write:

> Harry feels neglected and treated too much like a child, and gets jealous because his friends are made prefects and he is not, he claims all the merit for himself....So the temptation of being independent of all these gifts, of being autonomous and a great hero all by himself is strong for Harry and he succumbs to it at least temporarily.[17]

---

17   Wandinger, Nicolas, Christoph Drexler, and Teresa Peter, "Harry Potter and the Art of Theology I: A Theological Perspective on J.K. Rowling's Novels--Part One: Healing, Grace and Original Sin," *Milltown Studies* 52 (2003): 1-26.

In this way, Harry falls prey to the same sinful mindset as Voldemort: he is better off alone; he can succeed on his own, and he is better than others. This tactic rarely serves him well, but luckily, Harry is a protagonist who learns and grows, and by the end of the series, he fights alongside the other members of Dumbledore's Army. Together they weaken Voldemort's resources. Whether by killing Nagini, snuffing out Bellatrix Lestrange, or fighting an army of Death Eaters, they pave the way for Voldemort's death and the eradication of intolerance.

Even if they don't label it as a sin, the books certainly seem to highlight the dangers of isolation. But they don't stop there. The *Harry Potter* series also focuses attention on two other sins: sameness and the misuse of covenant. Let's look at sameness first. This is perhaps the most prominent sinful mindset in the series, because as we said earlier, the overarching conflict in the *Harry Potter* books concerns diversity. Voldemort does not believe in diversity while Dumbledore and his followers do. Voldemort wants to eradicate Muggles and Mudbloods, and he wants to purify the wizarding world in the same way that Hitler wanted to 'purify' the human world, while Dumbledore wants to ensure that the wizarding world is a place where pure-bloods, Mudbloods, Squibs, house-elves, and Muggles can peacefully co-exist and thrive. That Voldemort demands conformity and seeks to kill those who cannot conform is evidence of the extreme evils brought about by this sinful mindset.

That the many members of the wizarding world subscribed to Voldemort's ideology—although, to be fair, some were confunded—is evidence that this sin also has a corporate dimension to it. Many are responsible for the crimes carried out during Voldemort's reign either because they actively contributed as (Nicolas Wandinger)Death Eaters (i.e. Bellatrix Lestrange) or because they denied the truth for too long (Cornelius Fudge). The extent to which this sin infiltrates the wizarding world has dire consequences, leading to torture, death, and war. It is, without doubt, the paradigmatic sinful mindset of the series, and as a result, it leads to a majority of evils in the wizarding world.

While the conflict between Mudbloods and pure-bloods is clearly an example of the sin of sameness, other subplots show that this sin can also take other forms. For example, James and Sirius bully Snape because of his social awkwardness and his questionable fashion; they refuse to respect Snape for his own gifts and talents, instead discriminating against him simply because he is different. This treatment makes Snape resentful and drives him to his own exclusionary practices: he joins the Death Eaters and bears a lifelong grudge against James Potter and his friends because of their browbeating.

Likewise, the wizarding world enslaves house-elves because they are considered inferior, despite the fact that they have gifts of their own. One of the most compelling manifestations of this sin involves the relationship between Kreacher and Sirius Black. Sirius makes no secret of his dislike for Kreacher, treating the house-elf with disregard and contempt. In return, Kreacher betrays Sirius in a way that ultimately leads to Sirius's death. What this relationship between Kreacher and Sirius shows is the way in which sin is communicable, if not by birth then by exposure. Sirius's attitude and actions towards Kreacher cause him to become bitter and vengeful; he betrays Sirius precisely because Sirius has done little to endear himself, because their relationship is based on discrimination and not love or respect. As Dumbledore explains following his death, "Whatever Kreacher's faults, it must be admitted that Sirius did nothing to make Kreacher's lot easier...Indifference and neglect often do much more damage than outright dislike... We wizards have mistreated and abused our fellows for too long, and we are now reaping our reward" (*OP,* 832, 834).

Finally, we come to misusing the covenant as sin. In the early books of the Bible, God makes a covenant with the Israelite people, promising that they will be a chosen people if they remain loyal and obey the commandments. As there is no covenant in the *Harry Potter* series like the covenant God makes with humans in the biblical witness, it may seem hard to find a parallel, but I would like to suggest that there are laws and ethics that form a kind of covenant between members of the wizarding world and the principles of love. Witches and wizards agree to abide by these laws and mores, but the manner in which they uphold them sometimes destroys the covenant's intention. Dolores Umbridge is the most paradigmatic example of that: she interpreted laws and legalistic structures in a brutal way that ignored their true intent. She refused to acknowledge the spirit of love and compassion that guided the covenant of the wizarding world in her positions as Chief Inquisitor and Headmistress. She abused the structures of Hogwarts by passing decree after decree and abused students, quite literally, with her sadistic forms of punishment. Nor was Dolores Umbridge any more exemplary as Head of the Muggle-Born Registration Commission, where she used her power to sentence numerous innocent witches and wizards to Azkaban and the fate of the Dementors simply because of their parentage. Repeatedly, Dolores Umbridge failed to acknowledge the covenant of love and respect that Harry, Dumbledore and others recognized as fundamental to wizarding society.

The final example of sin I'd like to discuss is the misuse of human nature (#5). Recall that when humans misuse their nature, they disregard that they are embodied, social, and time-bound creatures. They fight against the reality that they live in a body with certain limitations, and by so doing, reject part of what it means to be human—to die. Voldemort exemplifies this sinful mindset perfectly. His desire to attain immortality shows an intention to override human nature, inclining him not only to this sin but also to the sin of pride.

The reader also notices that it is as if Voldemort wears the consequences of near immortality on his skin. As he makes each Horcrux, he loses his human features and becomes uglier, symbolizing that giving up one's humanity comes at a cost—all that is beautiful in a person withers away when he or she seeks such ends. Needless to say, the books clearly frown upon this kind of behavior, and it becomes one of the false idols Harry seeks to expose.

We also see a nod towards this sin in a more creative and nuanced way. Recall that in *The Prisoner of Azkaban*, Hermione uses a Time-Turner to attend her classes; at the end of the book, the Time-Turner gets used in a different way—to save Sirius and Buckbeak. During their adventure, Hermione explains to Harry that using the Time-Turner carries great risks because it alters something that ought to remain stable: time itself. Hermione explains the risk to Harry in this way:

> "Don't you understand? We're breaking one of the most important wizarding laws! Nobody's supposed to change time, nobody! You heard Dumbledore, if we're seen—"
>
> "We'd only be seen by ourselves and Hagrid!"
>
> "Harry, what do you think you'd do if you saw yourself bursting into Hagrid's house?" said Hermione.
>
> "I'd—I'd think I'd gone mad," said Harry, "or I'd think there was some Dark Magic going on—"
>
> "*Exactly!* You wouldn't understand, you might even attack yourself! Don't you see? Professor McGonagall told me what awful things have happened when wizards have meddled with time....Loads of them ended up killing their past or future selves by mistake!" (*PA*, 398-9)

What is interesting here is that Hermione has, throughout the book, altered time in a way that is sanctioned by the wizarding world, as if to say that the wizarding world seems to have a different standard when it comes to altering the basics of human existence than Christianity might.

Yet Hermione also tells Harry that in order to get a Time-Turner, Professor McGonagall, "had to write all sorts of letters to the Ministry of Magic so I could have one. She had to tell them that I was a model student, and that I'd never, ever use it for anything except my studies" (*PA*, 395-6). In other words, even the wizarding authorities are wary about tampering with something as fundamental as time; they recognize that it carries great risks for misuse, yet they do not condemn it outright. So while wizards do not view tampering with fundamental notions of reality like time as inherently wrong, they do recognize that altering them in certain ways is inappropriate. As a result, they know that such activities need to be closely monitored.

Now, I should be perfectly clear that Christians—as far as I know—do not consider time travel a sin, though truth be told I don't think any theologian has spent much time on the topic! So we have to be careful not to lend too much weight to this final example. What can be said is that both Christians and wizards seem to believe that there are aspects to our reality that are givens, and they're not intended to be tampered with. Both Christians and members of the wizarding world understand that human nature has limits, and that there are dire consequences when those limits are not heeded. So while the specific limits may be different—fallible bodies for humans and linear time for wizards—the principles guiding them are the same.

Conclusion

What we've seen in this chapter is that those flawed dispositions that Christians label as sins are mirrored by the behaviors and values of wizards. So though the term sin is never used in the series, we can see that both the wizarding world and theologians in the Christian world share similar values about how humans should exist in relation to God, themselves, and others.

In the classroom, this gives the philosophical understanding of sin a new dimension: sin is that which keeps people from living whole and full lives, and it is something so ingrained in our global psyche that it is as if we were born with it. My hope is that the term might help my students—regardless of whether they are Christian—to label some of the injustices they see both in the books and in the real world. By so doing, they may begin to realize that sin touches Harry's world as deeply as it touches our own.

Questions for Your Reflection

1)   Does the magical community have a similar response to guilt or shame regarding sin as some of my students did? How would a belief that all are sinners shape the wizarding world?

2)   Often in our world, sin begets sin. The sin of one person

can lead to the sin of another or the sin of one person may become deeper and more complicated over time. Does this happen in the *Harry Potter* series? If so, what are some examples where certain sins grow into a larger realm of sin?

3)   How is Harry's frequent gut reaction of going it alone to save the world different than the use of one's individual talents and gifts for a higher purpose? Where have we seen examples of the latter in the series?

4)   How is diversity represented in "groups of sameness?" Some examples are Gryffindor students, centaurs, and the Order of the Phoenix. Reflect on how sin plays out in Gryffindor groups. Is this different from how sin appears within the stringent laws of Slytherins?

5)   Umbridge's relation to the law is binding and stagnant, whereas, the commitment to love seems to be unpredictable and freeing. What are other examples of sin creating prisons and love producing freedom?

CHAPTER 4:

Who Really *Is* the Chosen One?

Christology

Meeting Christ in History

CHRISTIANS HAVE WORSHIPPED HIM, and academics have studied him. Throngs of seekers are intrigued by him. Tourists have flocked to his birthplace; archaeologists have searched for remnants for his tomb, and through prayer and visions, faithful Christians have developed relationships with Jesus for over 2,000 years. But though Jesus is one of the world's most compelling citizens, remarkably little is known about his life—none but Jesus' contemporaries could describe what he looked like, whether he had a good sense of humor, whether his voice was high-pitched or gravelly, or if he preferred figs to dates.

Theologians have much to ponder as well: from the dawn of Christianity onwards, they have sought to understand who Jesus would have to be in order to be the Messiah. Much of the most pivotal theological work was done in the early years of Christianity, in the patristic period. In this chapter, we will spend some time considering the debates of these patristic writers as well as the writings of the medieval female theologian Julian of Norwich. We will then see if anything like a Christ-figure is described in Rowling's writing.

But before turning to the theological debates concerning Jesus, it's important to have a general sense of who Jesus was in history. Scholars believe that he was born around the year 4 BCE in what is now present-day Israel and that he worked as a carpenter and rabbi. Jesus was Jewish, he spoke a language related to Hebrew known as Aramaic, and it is possible that he was able to read. At the time, Israel was part of the Roman Empire.

It is unclear how long his ministry lasted before his crucifixion: John's Gospel says that it lasted for approximately three years while Matthew, Mark, and Luke suggest that it was closer to only one. His brief work was characterized by a radical hospitality unknown in ancient times: he welcomed all to eat and talk with him, especially those that society shunned, such as tax collectors or prostitutes, and the gospel writers say that Jesus also healed the sick, even working on the Sabbath to do so, which was considered a violation of Jewish law. Around him he gathered a band of followers called disciples who traveled with him from town to town to help preach a message of hope and redemption. This message was rooted in Judaism but sought to amend what Jesus perceived to be problems with the practice of his faith.

But when Jesus came to preach and teach at the Temple in Jerusalem—which has since been destroyed—he ran into difficulty. His teachings drew criticism from authorities and as a result, he was arrested and tried before Pontius Pilate, a Roman procurator. Sentenced to death, Jesus is believed to have died in Jerusalem; Christians believe that his body was placed in a tomb, and three days after his death, he rose from the dead. Christians also traditionally believe that Jesus was crucified at age 33.

Jesus left no writings of his own. His quotations and the stories we have about him were recorded by a set of biographers who wrote in the years after his death—the gospel writers. Of these accounts, Mark's was the first to be written. It is the shortest gospel, and it seems throughout as if Mark is writing with a great sense of urgency and secrecy. Matthew and Luke, who both composed their accounts after Mark did, drew from Mark in their writing, as well as from another shared source, known as the Q source. Hence, when reading their accounts of Jesus' ministry, you can see that certain sections have been taken directly from Mark while others have been expanded or altered. Because these three gospels share similar sources, they are known as the synoptic gospels (you can purchase parallel editions of the gospels if you are interested in seeing exactly what passages and phrases the synoptic gospels share in common). In contrast, John's gospel did not draw from the same body of writing that the synoptic writers did. His is also the newest of the gospels chronologically, believed to have been composed at the conclusion of the first century CE.

Chart of Gospel Sources:

Gospel	Sources
Mark	Mark
Matthew	Mark, Q, Matthew
Luke	Mark, Q, Luke
John	John

When reading the four gospels, it is remarkable to see how each author has a unique tone and account of Jesus' life. In fact, there are only three stories common to all the gospels: the feeding of the five thousand, the cleansing of the Temple, and the concluding narrative concerning the end of Jesus' life. Moreover, each of the gospel writers depicts Jesus in a different way. For Mark, Jesus has a sense of urgency and intense energy, while Matthew highlights Jesus as the fulfillment of Old Testament prophecies. Luke's Jesus has a resigned, pastoral quality to him, and John's Jesus is the most self-reflective and self-aware of the portrayals.

Yet despite these differences, it is also remarkable to see how similar the overarching theme is: all the gospels recognize that there was something truly unique about Jesus—all of them portray him as a miracle worker, healer, teacher, prophet and redeemer. It was this last point that particularly interested the patristic writers. These early Christian theologians asked who Jesus would have to be in order to be the Christian savior, and their work evolved into some of the most fundamental tenets of Christianity, tenets that endure to this day.

The Patristic Authors

One of the goals of the earliest Christian theologians was to figure out the relationship between Jesus and God. That Jesus was human was clear—he could be killed after all—and yet, Jesus says that he is God's Son (i.e. Matt. 3:17). So what does that mean and, in turn, what did the relationship between God and Jesus look like?

Before we read a bit about these authors, it is important to realize two things: first, debates about Christology (who Jesus is) did not stop with these authors. This discussion continues to this day and is an enduring one amongst theologians. Yet that said, the work of the patristic writers came to inform later theologians, becoming the building blocks for Christian thought. The idea that Jesus is both God and man, for instance, originated through these writers, as did the doctrine of the Trinity, the idea that God exists as Father, Son, and Holy Spirit. These three conceptions of God are said to be unique entities but also united as one, kind of like a plaid skirt—the skirt might be made up of red, blue, and green threads, but they are so interwoven that they cannot be separated. While we won't be talking about the Trinity much here, understanding it can help a great deal when reading about Christology because it gives a sense of where the work of these theologians will ultimately wind up.

To bring this debate to life, let's imagine that these early theologians are participating in a metaphorical chess tournament. Strategy in the game will revolve around trying to make sense of biblical verses such as this one from the Gospel of John: "And the Word became flesh and lived among us, and we have seen his glory, the glory as of a father's only son, full of grace and truth" (Jn. 1:14).

As you read this section, you will see how the debates build upon each other—this is why the rounds are done as a tournament, even though they don't strictly match the definition of 'tournament' because the winner doesn't personally advance from one round to the next. Instead, it is the *ideas* of the winner that proceed to the next game.

The Quarter-Finals:

The Ebionites vs. the Docetists. The Ebionites suggested that Jesus was only human and not divine. The strength of their strategy—what got put in the suitcase—comes from the biblical witness, especially from Mark's gospel, where it is clear that Jesus is human because he suffers, he dies, and he loses his temper. Yet their greatest strength was also their greatest vulnerability, for that same biblical witness states that Jesus was God (i.e. John 1:14).

Matched against the Ebionites, we have an able opponent in the form of the Docetists. The Docetists believed that Jesus' body was an illusion and that he was something like a divine ghost on earth. In this mindset, Jesus was not fully human but rather only seemed to be human. (Appropriately enough, the word Docetist comes from the Greek, which means, "to seem.") The Ebionites and the Docetists are thus ably matched: the Docetist's strength is the Ebionite's weakness and vice versa.

At the conclusion of this match, there is no clear winner because the flaws in each group's views are too great to overlook. The biblical witness simply cannot be reconciled with their logic, and so neither of them comes to prevail in Christian thought. However, these two groups do make a lasting contribution because they framed the matches of future theologians in terms of Jesus' humanity and divinity.

The Semi-Finals:

As we saw in the quarter-finals, the contest was between thinkers who believed Jesus was fully human and those who thought Jesus was something of a godly ghost. But if Jesus is neither of these things, then what does Jesus share with God? This will be the focus of the semi-final game, where Arius and Athanasius will compete to see exactly what Jesus has in common with God.

Arius vs. Athanasius: Arius has the distinction of being the source of the first great Christian controversy, known as the Arian controversy. Arius was trying to be clear about the distinction between Jesus and God, but he was also mindful of the failures of the Ebionites and the Docetists. Jesus was neither totally human nor totally divine in Arius's thought; rather, Jesus was a kind of perfect human who ranked above others and might even be seen as a sort of lesser divine figure. Arius insisted that Jesus and God were not the same, and in order to show that, he says that Jesus was made by God, which made him a "creature" just like any other creature on earth, be it human, fish, toad, flower, etc. As we will see, the term "creature" is going to figure prominently in the match.

There is one other prominent way in which Arius demonstrates that Jesus and God are not the same being nor do they have the same status: this has to do with Jesus' use of the term "Son of God." Arius writes that when Jesus says in the gospels that he is God's "Son," he meant this metaphorically to show the special relationship that existed between God and himself. But that is the extent of their union: Jesus and God may have a unique way of relating to one another, but nonetheless, they are different entities: God is the Creator, and Jesus is a product of that creation.

Like the Ebionite's, Arius's greatest theological strength were those biblical passages that highlighted Jesus' humanity. But Arius made a couple of bad offensive moves in his chess game that his opponent Athanasius was quick to notice:

1. One of the most important characteristics of being a "creature" is that a creature can't do the work of salvation, otherwise humans could save other humans. Only the creator can do this. (Remember this principle! We're going to say much more about it when we come to the chapter on salvation.) But if Jesus is a creature, then Jesus isn't in a position to save humans. Yet the New Testament is clear that Jesus is the Messiah. Therefore, Arius was wrong and Jesus cannot be a creature.

2. Christians worship Jesus, but if Jesus was a creature, then humans wouldn't be worshipping God but part of creation. This would mean that standard Christian practices would actually be idolatrous

Check mate! Arius was the big loser in this match because Athanasius's arguments forced Arius into a corner from which he could not back out. Athanasius's views eventually prevailed at a meeting of church leaders at Nicaea, where it was decided that Jesus and God the Father were of equal status and shared the same substance (in Greek, *homoousios*).

Is all of this discussion of the relation between Father and Son making some lights go off when you think of *Harry Potter*? Hold those thoughts a bit longer. Once we know more about the relationship between Father and Son in Christian thought, we'll be able to give a full analysis of whether a similar relationship exists in the books.

The Final Round:

The match between Arius and Athanasius centered on what Jesus and God the Father shared in common, and it was decided that they must be united in an intimate way—they must share the same substance. But what exactly does it mean for Jesus to share the substance of God and yet still be a human? This will be the focus of the final match, in which you will find that a disproportionate number of the players have names that begin with the letter A!

The Alexandrian theologians vs. the Antiochian theologians. Apollinaris was an acquaintance of Athanasius and like Athanasius, he was from the Alexandrian school of thought—didn't I say there were a lot of A's? He dealt with the theological question of how Jesus could be both human and divine by suggesting that Jesus had a human body but a divine mind. His theological strength was that he clearly showed how God and humanity could exist separately within the same person. But what he left out of the suitcase was that Christians believed sin didn't just affect the body—it affected the entire person. In the Apollinarian framework, it was easy to assume that if only Jesus' body was human, then only the body was saved.

The Antiochians instead said that Jesus had two natures—divine and human—that existed together in one person. This meant that Jesus was both fully human and fully divine, all in the same bodily frame. Their framework sent an effective jab at Apollinaris because the Antiochans suggested a way for both the body and mind to be saved. But their theological vulnerability was this: it was easy to separate out the two natures so that it looked like Jesus had a split personality instead of being a single, unified person.

The conclusion to this match is more complicated than the others because in this particular game, replacements stepped in to correct the errors of the previous players. After Apollinaris's errors were pointed out, Cyril of Alexandria took his place in representing the Alexandrians. Cyril said that the human and divine were so united in Jesus that though these two different natures existed within Jesus, they shared each other's properties. That meant that the human part of Jesus could perform miracles because the humanity and divinity were so closely linked together, which is different from what the Antiochians were saying. To explain the difference, imagine a blank canvas, which we will say is a metaphor for Jesus. Blue paint represents Jesus' divinity; yellow represents his humanity. On the Alexandrian canvas, the blue and yellow paints would be mixed together to create green. While blending the colors together does allow for a truly intimate mixture, the danger is that the individuality of each is compromised—blue and yellow disappear in order to create the new color. On the Antiochian canvas, blue and yellow are painted side-by-side, next to each other but not mixing. This preserves the distinction between the two colors but makes it seem as if they are completely separate from one another.

It is tough to call the winner of this match. Eventually, the debate between these two schools of thought got so intense that it was addressed at another council of religious leaders—the Council of Chalcedon, which took place in 451. This Council issued a statement that was intended to accommodate both Alexandrians and Antiochians. As one theological textbook explains:

It was declared [at Chalcedon] that Jesus Christ is "fully human and fully divine...existing in two natures... without confusion, without change, without division, without separation." "Without confusion and without change" warned the Alexandrians that to think of Jesus as having one nature—a "mixture" of divinity and humanity—is problematic. Such a being is neither fully human nor fully divine and therefore cannot be "God with us." "Without division and without separation" advised the Antiochians not to "compartmentalize" the two natures of Christ, as though they had nothing to do with one another. Such extreme separation could only render impossible the believers' shared hope that God has assumed the human condition in the person of Christ.[18]

Though Chalcedon was meant to pacify both Alexandrians and Antiochians, many were not satisfied with the Council's conclusions: the most extreme Alexandrians and Antiochians split off from the majority of Christians, who affirmed Chalcedon. The Antiochian Christians went on to become prominent in the Eastern world, spreading as far as China, while the Alexandrians were prominent in North Africa and the Middle East; during the rise of Islam, many of them converted.

And so we conclude our journey into the patristic debate about who Jesus Christ is. As we said earlier, it would be incorrect to say that the debates ceased after Chalcedon—they continue to the present day to be a point of contention between theologians and denominations. However, as Christian history progressed, the discussion began to shift away from focusing on who Jesus was in relation to God and instead began to focus on what it meant for Jesus to be a savior. We will return to that question in the chapter on salvation, but in the meantime, let's talk a little bit about Christology in the Harry Potter series before we discuss our last theologian, Julian of Norwich.

18   Baker-Fletcher, Karen, et. al, "Jesus Christ," *Constructive Theology: A Contemporary Approach to Classical Themes*, ed. Serene Jones and Paul Lakeland (Minneapolis: Fortress Press, 2005) 168 9.

Patristic Christology and *Harry Potter*

Let's begin by asking this very big question: is there anyone in the books that might match the Chalcedonian image of Christ as fully human and fully divine? Two characters present themselves as clear frontrunners: Dumbledore and Harry.

We will consider Dumbledore first. Rowling makes the reader believe Dumbledore has divine characteristics—in the early books, at least. Like God, Dumbledore has larger-than-life status: as the only person who Voldemort fears, he seems to have virtually limitless power, abundant kindness, and infinite knowledge. At the end of the first book, for instance, Harry tells Ron and Hermione that he felt Dumbledore had a reason for letting him and his friends defeat Voldemort. He says, "I think he knows more or less everything that goes on here, you know. I reckon he had a pretty good idea we were going to try [to prevent Voldemort from getting the stone], and instead of stopping us, he just taught us enough to help." (*SS*, 302). This is just one of many moments when Dumbledore seems to know more than a mortal should, and so it is easy for us to come to believe that he is intended to be Christ-like.

Indeed, John Granger has also commented about the similarities between Christ and Dumbledore at length in his beloved Hogwarts Professor blog. In addition to drawing parallels between Christ in Gethsemane and Dumbledore's drinking of the goblet in *Half-Blood Prince*, he also remarks upon more general personality traits that the two share in common. He writes that like Jesus, Dumbledore descries discrimination and cares for those society shuns:

> Dumbledore is on good terms with house-elves, centaurs, and goblins. He is even able to parley with the giants through Hagrid and Madame Maxime because of his good reputation among the giants. He sees the crisis in the wizarding world with Lord Voldemort largely as crows coming home to roost for the prejudices of the Wizarding world against magical creatures.

He also adopts those the world would not. Remus Lupin, boy werewolf, is admitted to Hogwarts and later even given a job as the Defense Against the Dark Arts teacher despite wizard prejudice against his affliction. Hagrid, too, is trusted and respected by Dumbledore despite his being half-giant. Muggle-born wizards and witches, Half-Bloods, and Pure Blood families are all treated by the Headmaster without distinction or prejudice except in the light of their respective virtues and vices born of their choices rather than their blood lines. Snape, if not a half-vampire, then as certainly no Little Lord Fauntleroy, is also an Albus adoptee. In being "no respecter of persons," Dumbledore thinks as God thinks, not as men think.[19]

Like God, Dumbledore has larger-than-life status: as the only person who Voldemort fears, he seems to have virtually limitless power, abundant kindness, and seemingly infinite knowledge. To give just one example, at the end of the first book, Dumbledore was supposed to be in London, far from Hogwarts, when Harry put his life in danger to find the sorcerer's stone. Yet at the last moment, Dumbledore returned to the school, somehow knowing the peril his student was in. "No sooner had I reached London," he says, "Than it became clear to me that the place I should be was the one I had just left" (*SS*, 297). This is just one of many moments when Dumbledore seems to know more than a mortal should, and so it is easy for us to come to believe that he is intended to be God-like.

If Dumbledore's divinity seems obvious throughout these early books, we begin to see evidence of Dumbledore's humanity as the series progresses. Like Jesus, Dumbledore is subject to the weaknesses of his body: as we see in the sixth book, his hand is incurably wounded, and later he dies. But while Dumbledore may exhibit characteristics of both the humanity and divinity that are evident in Jesus, the big question

19   John Granger, *Hogwarts Professor: Dumbledore a Christ Figure in Half-Blood Prince?*, 15 July 2009, 10 January 2010 <http://www.hogwartsprofessor.com/is-dumbledore-a-christ-figure-in-half-blood-prince/ Accessed January 28, 2010. >.

is whether he is *too* human: one of the things that I didn't mention earlier is that most Christian theologians believe that even though Jesus was human, he was a human without sin—hence, it says in 1 Peter 2:22 that Jesus, "Committed no sin, and no deceit was found in his mouth." (As we will see in the chapter on salvation, this is one of the reasons Jesus was in a position to save humanity.)

So while Dumbledore's bodily frailty does not conflict with classical Christianity's conception of Christ, the sins he commits in his life do—his friendship with Grindelwald causes him to be selfish and blind to the needs of others; his quest for the Deathly Hallows, as we explored earlier, is a display of sinful pride, as is the hope for a wizarding revolution. And while there are theologians who have proposed Christologies that afford Jesus the capacity to sin, these are rare and have the difficulty of fighting for validity against 2000 years of theological tradition (for more on the interplay between reason and tradition, turn to the Revelation chapter!).

Given all of this, it seems unlikely that Dumbledore is the Christ-figure in the series. So from here, let's turn to the possibility that Harry might fit the bill. Like Dumbledore, Harry seems to possess certain qualities that make him like Jesus—that he is the "Chosen One," destined to sacrifice himself for the wizarding world, might be similar to God's words at Jesus' baptism: "This is my Son, the Beloved, with whom I am well pleased" (Matt. 3:17). Additionally, his sacrifice, as we will see later, certainly echoes Jesus'.

But is Harry truly God and truly human? As with Dumbledore, it is difficult to make this argument, because like Dumbledore, the analogy between Harry and Jesus is limited by Harry's fallibility. He is prone to jealousy and secretiveness, and as we've said earlier, his tendency towards independence cost Sirius his life. Moreover, unlike Dumbledore, Harry does not possess the kind of knowledge and power characteristic of the Christian God, which means he reads as fully human but not fully divine.

Yet in Harry's defense, there is a way in which we could argue that he, like Dumbledore, is not a perfect analogy but is still a Christ-like character. In Harry's case, this has to do with his relationship to Ron and Hermione. Recall how Jesus is part of the Trinity, the three in one and one in three. Likewise, Harry may be a complete human being with his own gifts and personality, but he could only complete the mission set for him with the help of two friends with complementary gifts— Ron with his loyalty and Hermione with her brains. It would be difficult to press this analogy too hard, because neither Ron nor Hermione perfectly represent either God the Father (the creator) or God the Holy Spirit (the sustainer and spirit of the Church). But again, the relationship Harry has with Ron and Hermione might well constitute a loose analogy between these three characters and the Christian Trinity, not a tight bind. Like the Trinitarian God, the three friends are united at a deep level, and just as Jesus came into his own through his relationship to the Father and the Holy Spirit, so Harry is given the tools and gifts he needs to attain salvation for the wizarding world through his relationship to Ron and Hermione.

What we see here is that neither of these classical conceptions of Jesus fit perfectly with the possibilities in the *Harry Potter* series. Though both Dumbledore and Harry share some of the characteristics of the Christian Messiah, it is hard to see clear parallels in either. But we still have one theologian left to consider, one who adds a new layer of Jesus' identity to the discussion.

Julian of Norwich

Julian's writings about Jesus take a very different twist than the other writers we've already discussed and her views are not as well-represented in Christian tradition. If the patristic authors are all lemons, Julian might be a lime: both are in the citrus family but the flavors are quite different.

Julian was a medieval mystic and theologian who lived during the late fourteenth and early fifteenth centuries. She spent her life in Norwich, England where she was an anchoress, a woman who lived in a cell attached to the village church. The cell, known as an anchorhold, had no door, so it was it was impossible for her to leave. However, it did have two small windows: one faced the inside of the church, so that she could receive communion and watch the service. The second window faced the outside world, so that she could meet with visitors and give spiritual guidance to them; she also received meals in this manner. Julian, like other anchoresses and anchorites (the male equivalent) chose to live her life this way so she could spend a most of her time in contemplative prayer.

When Julian was thirty years old, she became seriously ill and believed she was dying. At the height of her illness, Julian saw a series of visions of Jesus, and she recorded them after her recovery. *The Shewings of Julian of Norwich*, also known as *Revelations of Divine Love*, is believed to be the first English book written by a woman, and you may be familiar with its most famous phrase: "All shall be well, all shall be well, and all manner of thing shall be well." It is alluded to in the last line of *Deathly Hallows*: "The scar had not pained Harry for nineteen years. All was well" (759).

What is unique about Julian, at least at the time in which she was writing, is that she paints a portrait of Jesus as the mother of humans. Just as God the Creator has the qualities of a father, Julian suggested that Jesus has the qualities of a mother. This is not to say that Jesus was biologically female, but rather to say that the best metaphor for understanding who Jesus was is the metaphor of a mother. She writes that, "The kind, loving mother who knows and recognizes the needs of her child, she watches over it most tenderly, as the nature and condition of motherhood demands. And as it grows in age her actions change, although her love does not…Thus he [Jesus] is our natural mother."[20]

Julian's use of the word mother frames the Christological discussion not in terms of the relationship between Jesus and God, as the patristic authors did. Rather, Julian is interested in who Jesus is in relation to real people. Her image of mothering makes Jesus into the head of a "universal nursery" full of "spiritual infants and toddlers" as contemporary philosopher of religion Marilyn McCord Adams writes. She goes on to explain that for Julian, "Jesus provides the loving personal environment

---

20   Julian of Norwich, *Revelations of Divine Love*, trans. Elizabeth Spearing (New York: Penguin Books, 1998). 142.

in which we are always enfolded, before and whether we are actually aware of it or not."[21]

Julian's image also shows the role Jesus plays in a human being's development: Jesus helps people to grow into mature and healthy selves, and even in sufferings like Julian's illness, Jesus will be the nurturer.

Julian's Jesus in *Harry Potter*

Since Julian places so much emphasis upon Jesus' role as mother, perhaps we should look at the possibility that a mother might be the Jesus-figure in the series. We're going to look at one in particular, and it may come as no surprise to you that the candidate is Lily Potter. We know very little about Lilly's character compared to other characters in the series, yet there are certain aspects of Harry's mother that might qualify her as Christ-like, especially in light of Julian of Norwich's writings. Like Julian of Norwich's Jesus, Lily is a mother not only to Harry but to the entire wizarding world because through her love the wizarding world is saved from Voldemort, at least for awhile. Moreover, like the mothering Jesus Julian describes, Lilly is a nurturing presence who appears consistently throughout the series at the times that Harry yearns for her most—i.e., when Harry is surrounded by a community of the dead at the end of *Deathly Hallows*, it seems to be Lily's support that matters most and her presence that sustains Harry as he walks to his own end. With her help, even death does not seem overwhelming. Rowling writes that,

> Lily's smile was widest of all. She pushed her long hair
> back as she drew close to him, and her green eyes,
> so like his, searched his face hungrily, as though she
> would never be able to look at him enough.

> "You've been so brave."

> He could not speak. His eyes feasted on her, and he

---

21   Adams, Marilyn McCord, *Christ and Horrors: The Coherence of Christology*. Cambridge: Cambridge University Press, 2006. 160.

thought that he would like to stand and look at her forever, and that would be enough (699).

As Harry walks to his death, it is his mother, more than anyone else, that he wants by his side, and it seems that the sheer power of his mother's love makes even the greatest challenge possible to bear. Like Julian's Jesus, Lily's role in Harry's life is one that gives love and nurturing support, and she gives it abundantly.

Lily also possesses some of the God-human characteristics of the patristic writers: she certainly seems to be all-good, especially given that her capacity to love is so powerful that it protects Harry for seventeen years. She also is potentially all-knowing insofar as she realized what she needed to do to protect her son. Like Harry and Dumbledore, she too is fully human, with the capacity to suffer and die, yet she lacks the major character flaws and inclinations to sin we see in those two. Yet as we will see in the next chapter on sacrifice, there are substantial reasons why Lily is not a perfect analogy to Christ.

So without further adieu, let us move on to that discussion!

Questions for Your Reflection

1) Are there any other potential Christ figures in the series? Who are they and why?
2) What is the distinction between the Christ figure and a Christ-like figure? How does that tension play out in the series?
3) Is a human non-divine Jesus attractive? Is a God non-human Jesus attractive? Why or why not? How does your opinion shape your thoughts on Christ figures in the Harry Potter series?
4) What additional details in the life of Christ would be helpful to understand who can be a Christ-figure?
5) How is James' sacrifice different than Lily's?

CHAPTER 5:

Walking Towards Death's Arms

Sacrifice

Taking the Bull by its Horns

A T THE END OF *Half-Blood Prince*, Harry and Dumbledore traveled to a cave, hoping to find another Horcrux, when they discovered that an unconventional toll was needed to gain entrance: blood. Harry offered to make the payment, but Dumbledore wouldn't let him, saying, "Your blood is worth more than mine," (*HBP*, 560). Dumbledore then cut his hand and smeared his blood upon the cavern wall in order to gain entrance to the inner sanctum.

This becomes just one example of how characters in *Harry Potter* make self-offerings or sacrifices. They take different guises and purposes, but as we will see, many of them share aspects of Jesus' self-offerings.

When I started relaying the ideas in this chapter to my students, one of the most important points I wanted to drive home was how powerful and transformative sacrifice can be. This is often not a natural reaction in our culture—when you think sacrifice, what comes to mind? Ancient rituals? The slaying of goats and cows? The phrase, "Who does *that* anymore?"

It often seems like sacrifice has become a dirty word in our culture. We associate it with superstition, think slaughtering animals to please the gods is barbaric, and cannot imagine how sacrifice is relevant to our lives today. How many of us could imagine giving up our luxuries, our money, or our lives as payment for a debt to God? We would prefer a kinder, gentler God or, at the very least, a kinder, gentler way of paying our heavenly bills!

But within Jewish and Christian thought, sacrifice has a long, vibrant history that has often been misunderstood. In what follows, I will discuss the history of Jewish and Christian sacrifice and show the way in which these ideas have made their way into J.K. Rowling's writing.

Jewish Understanding of Sacrifice

Like many other concepts in Christianity, it's hard to understand what Christians mean by sacrifice without looking at the Jewish tradition. To do that, we have to go back to the Book of Leviticus, the book of the Hebrew Bible that outlines the code priests used to practice rituals and sacrifices. The first seven chapters of Leviticus outline some of the most common forms of Jewish sacrifices. These sacrifices can be roughly divided into three groups:

1. **Gift Offerings:** Offerings of vegetables and animals given in thanks for God's work.
2. **Meal Offerings:** Animals, without the fat, that were eaten by the one who made the offering. These were given in thanksgiving for health or wholeness, such as when a woman who had given birth returned to well-being.
3. **Sin Offerings:** Animal offerings, with fat, that were consumed by priests in the Temple. They were given to attain forgiveness from sins.[22]

What is interesting about these offerings is while different materials were sacrificed at different times of day and for different reasons, all were offered using fire. The burning

---

22   Dunnill, John "Communicative Bodies and Economies of Grace: The Role of Sacrifice in the Christian Understanding of the Body." *Journal of Religion.* Vol. 83, No. 1. 2003. 85.

produced smoke that rose to the heavens and was said to emit a "pleasing odor to the Lord" (Lev. 1:17; 2:9). That smoke literally brought God closer to the people who made the sacrifice, creating a space for God to enter their lives. The ability to be in intimate relationship with God through the smoke shows that the animal or grain offered to God was only a vehicle that created an opportunity for divine-human interaction. The offering didn't ultimately connect God to the sacrificer— the smoke did. Through the smoke, the offerer could reach the heart of the Jewish tradition: to be at one with God.

These ancient sacrifices were not trivial. Most people only owned a couple of animals and a small portion of land, so forfeiting a goat, dove, or cake of grain was impressive. To give up one cow when you only own a couple is a huge loss—imagine giving up thirty or sixty percent of your savings as an offering to God. And we think tithing is harsh!

In addition to these individual sacrifices there was a communal sacrifice offered once a year that covered all the sins of the Jewish people. This offering involved several sacrifices made by the High Priest on the Day of Atonement, or *Yom Kippur*. The High Priest would begin by slaughtering a bull and putting its blood into a bowl. Then he would choose two goats; one was offered to the Lord and the second became a scapegoat, quite literally—that's where the term comes from. The High Priest would place his hands upon this goat and say a prayer that transferred all the sins of the Jewish people onto it. Then the goat was led into the wilderness, and the High Priest entered the Holy of Holies—the room where God was thought to dwell—in the Temple in Jerusalem and scattered the blood of a slaughtered bull.

The practice of sacrifices like these may seem foreign to us because they ended long ago in Judaism. They began to alter following the destruction of the First Temple because the Jewish people were sent into exile and with no temple, there was no place to offer a sacrifice. So over time, slaughtering animals and giving grain to the Lord ceased altogether and were replaced by self-offerings of time or money. Likewise, the modern day *Yom Kippur* service is a day of fasting and prayer.

Though unfamiliar to us, these sacrificial rites were still

alive in some form during the establishment of Christianity, and in these rituals, especially those from the Day of Atonement, Judaism and Christianity met. The early Christian writers believed Jesus' sacrifice had a power beyond all of the Jewish offerings, especially those made on the Day of Atonement. The writer of the Letter to the Hebrews most clearly makes this comparison:

> But when Jesus came as a high priest of the good things that have come, then through the greater perfect tent (not made with hands, that is, not of creation), he entered once for all into the Holy Place, not with the blood of goats and calves, but with his own blood, thus obtaining eternal redemption. For if the blood of goats and bulls, with the sprinkling of the ashes of a heifer, sanctifies those who have been defiled so that their flesh is purified, how much more will the blood of Christ, who through the eternal Spirit offered himself without blemish to God, purify our conscience from dead works to worship the living God! (Heb. 9:11-14)

As the writer of Hebrews explains, Christ's sacrifice was so all-encompassing that it purified the conscience of humanity, freeing people to understand their relationship with God in a new way. So as in Judaism, the sacrifice itself is not an end. Rather, sacrifice is a means to transform the relationship that people have with God.

The writer of Hebrews is also clear in the book about two other things: first, Jesus' sacrifice creates a new covenant between humans and God that redeems them from the power of death (9:15), and second, Jesus' sacrifice was so powerful that it need only be done once, unlike the high priest's sacrifice, which was repeated annually (9:25-6). Hence, it is said that Jesus' sacrifice is a "once for all" sacrifice that encompasses all sins for all times. Nothing beyond it is needed.

Before we look at how two Christian thinkers interpreted Jesus' sacrifice, I want to add an important disclaimer. Based upon writings like the quotation from Hebrews, one may be tempted to say that Christianity is superior to Judaism or that it only reached its fulfillment because of Jesus. I strongly discourage this kind of reading. Instead, bear in mind that religions are not static. They are flexible and evolve. That is part of their nature because that is part of our nature.

By being flexible, religions avoid becoming stale or irrelevant, instead becoming meaningful in ways that resonate with the time and culture in which they exist. How Judaism was practiced three thousand years ago differs from how it is practiced today, and the birth and growth of Christianity was part of that evolution. What Christian thinkers have done is to reinterpret Jewish writings for their own time and place until these reinterpretations solidified into a new religion. This new religion is not necessarily better or worse than the old one, rather it is simply different, offering a new language to help people foster a fulfilling relationship with God.

Christian Thinkers on Sacrifice

Before looking at sacrifice in the *Harry Potter* books, I'd like to draw attention to two Christian writers on sacrifice—Anselm of Canterbury and René Girard. Anselm's satisfaction theory has become one of the most formational Christian ideas while René Girard's theory about the role of scapegoating provides a more recent but provocative take on sacrifice. These two writers, who lived hundreds of years apart from one another, had very different ideas about the purpose of sacrifice in Christianity, and because their ideas differ so greatly, they are an illuminating contrast to one another.

• Anselm of Canterbury's Satisfaction Theory

Anselm of Canterbury was a medieval theologian who lived from 1033 to 1109, and his writings are known for their logical rigor and attention to detail. Many of his tracts became foundational to Christian thought, and the one we will be focusing on is *Cur Deus Homo*, which translated means *Why the God-Man?* The goal of this tract was to explain why it was that Jesus needed to sacrifice himself, and why Jesus had to be both God and Man to do it. We've already seen a bit of this discussion in the chapter on Christ's identity, but what we'll see here is the way in which the writings of those earlier theologians began to seep into the Christian understanding of sacrifice.

Here's the gist of Anselm's thought: Anselm began by saying that both humans and God have a problem. On the human side, people were called to obey God but because of sin, they have not obeyed that call and die as a punishment (recognize Augustine here?). Over time, they accumulated a debt to God, a debt they cannot pay because they would need to live perfect, sinless lives in order to do so, and they cannot live perfect lives because they are tainted by sin. What a bind.

God's problem is different: God committed to love creation and wanted to forgive the sins of humanity but was also committed to the ideals of justice. If God forgave humanity's debt, it would violate the code of justice that required death as a punishment for the magnitude of human sin and disobedience.

So God and humanity find themselves in a quandary: humans were the ones who needed to pay the debt, but only God was in a position to do so because humans were tainted by sin. (As we saw in the Christology chapter, this was one of the reasons Arius was deemed a heretic: creatures aren't in a position to save another creature.) Then God comes up with an answer to this problem: Jesus, the God-Man. Jesus was able to both satisfy God's justice and have the ability to do it by being fully human and fully divine. Cleverly, this was accomplished through Jesus living a sinless life, so that he did not owe God a debt, not even the punishment of death. Yet Jesus agreed to be obedient to death on the cross, and by making that sacrifice, God was now in debt to Jesus. God agreed to cancel humanity's debt as payment to Jesus, and hence, God paid the debt without a violation of justice.

Anselm's theology is considered an elegant execution of logic, but only if one buys into the claim that humanity owes an unpayable debt to a God who will not relinquish a very defined code of justice. This goes back to some of the material we covered in the evil and sin chapters—only if we conceive humans and God in a certain way does Anselm hold up. If we said, for instance, that humans are not responsible for being in a state of sin, as Hick and Iranaeus might, or said that the Fall was fortunate, then it would be hard to argue that humans owe a debt for something they didn't do on purpose and that can be to their benefit.

• René Girard and Scapegoating

Earlier in this chapter, I discussed the role of the scapegoat in the ancient rituals of *Yom Kippur*. The twentieth century French philosopher René Girard picked up on the image of a scapegoat in his own writings on sacrifice, suggesting that Jesus was a very unique kind of scapegoat.

Girard begins by saying that humans have an instinct to imitate one another, and because humans imitate the same thing, they wind up desiring the same thing. The problem is that there are limited quantities of what's desired, which means not everyone will get what they want. You've probably seen this principle at work if you have a younger sibling—you may remember from your childhood that your sibling wanted to copy everything you did to the point of annoyance. Say you loved your Cabbage Patch Kid, Transformer, or Dora the Explorer doll, so naturally your little sibling wanted to play with it, too. But there was only one such doll in the house, so fighting arose when you and your sibling both wanted it. Perhaps you called your sibling names, perhaps you threatened to tell your mother, or perhaps, as happened to me when I was four, you got your hair pulled out. This is exactly the kind of thing Girard is referring to: he believes that violence erupts when many people desire the same thing but there are limited quantities of it.

Girard believes that this is a universal phenomena that dates back to the origin of humanity, so in order to avoid constant bickering and fights, humans decided early on take out their violent instincts on a scapegoat, an innocent that had no part in the conflict, like the goat on the Day of Atonement. Hurting the scapegoat gave violence a time and place, putting it into a box so that humans could unite over their hatred of the scapegoat instead of divide over unfulfillable desires. This created less overall violence and a greater sense of community.[23]

---

23   For a stunning and extremely disturbing example of scapegoating in our own times, see Freidoune Sahebjam's book, *The Stoning of Soraya M.*

Girard suggests that Jesus too was a scapegoat, but of a very different variety. Until Jesus, the cycle of scapegoating went uncritiqued and was an accepted practice. But Girard says that when God became human in Jesus, this mechanism was revealed because Jesus' sacrifice was intended to show the horror of what humanity was doing to itself when it yearned for inappropriate things.

Yet all too often in Christianity's history, this message fell on deaf ears—the Christian history of desiring the wrong things and scapegoating others, especially the Jewish people, continues to this day. It is Girard's hope that Christians will eventually recognize the way in which Jesus' sacrifice calls them to a new way of life.

Sacrifice in the *Harry Potter* series

Sacrifice is key in the *Harry Potter* series, and many characters sacrifice themselves for different reasons and to different ends. But do these sacrifices reflect anything about the Christian worldview? That is the question that we shall be asking here. Because so many characters sacrifice themselves in the books, it would be impossible to discuss them all, so I have selected those that are particularly interesting in relation to our topic. These sacrifices will be divided into three categories: once for all sacrifices, repeatable sacrifices, and ambiguous sacrifices. Let's begin with the first.

• Harry and the Once For All Sacrifice

When we think sacrifice in the wizarding world, we think Harry. So without further delay, let's get straight to heart of sacrifice in the series and look at that event. At the end of book seven, Harry walks to his death, knowing that he must forfeit his life so that the Horcrux which lies within him can be destroyed. After years of thinking that he could defeat Voldemort, Harry discovers the irony that the demise of his enemy can only occur if he dies. That knowledge leaves Harry stunned but sure of his fate:

Finally, the truth. Lying with his face pressed into the dusty carpet of the office where he had once thought he was learning the secrets of victory, Harry understood at last that he was not supposed to survive. His job was to walk calmly into Death's welcoming arms. Along the way, he was to dispose of Voldemort's remaining links to life, so that when at last he flung himself, the end would be clean, and the job that ought to have been done in Godric's Hollow would be finished: Neither would live, neither could survive (*DH*, 691).

Harry's acceptance of his fate bears striking similarities to Jesus' understanding of his own death. Praying to God in the dead of night in the Garden of Gethsemane, Jesus too recognizes that he must submit to death in order to accomplish the work of salvation.[24] Contemporary theologian Nikolaus Wandinger is therefore right to recognize the parallels that exist between Harry and Jesus in this moment:

> If there is any parallel to Gethsemani [*sic*] in *Harry Potter*, it is this scene, where Harry feels betrayed and abandoned by his longtime mentor Dumbledore, where he sees that the next logical step for him is to walk to his own death and yet trembles at this prospect, and the possibility of fleeing crosses his mind. The Gospels tell us that Jesus was motivated to go on by his unswerving obedience to the Father's will…It is the thoughts of his friends, the people he loved, who risked and lost their lives for him, and the danger that remains to his remaining friends, as long as Voldemort's reign is not broken, that drive him [Harry]. Thus in short, it is love and care for the life of others that motivates Harry

---

24   I am indebted to one of my former students, Amanda McAuliffe, for teaching me about how this moment in book seven relates to the Mormon interpretation of Gethsemane, which holds that the distress Jesus experienced in the Garden is the greatest psychological trial of his earthly life. It is my sense that that analyzing Jesus' struggles in the Garden of Gethsemane and Harry's struggle to walk to his own death would be a fruitful avenue of research for those whose expertise is Mormon theology.

to go along the path to his death, or put differently: he is prepared to sacrifice himself in order to avoid more people being sacrificed for him.[25]

Wandinger brings up an important point here: while both Harry and Christ's sacrifices are ones of obedience and love, it is clear at this point in the story that Harry's intention is to save his friends, and his death is an unfortunate necessity that must occur for Voldemort to die. In contrast, Christians believe that Christ died not only for his friends but also his enemies.

But as Wandinger points out, by the time that Voldemort dies it seems as if Harry, like Christ, cares about the welfare of his enemies. In the final battle, Harry says to Voldemort, "But before you try to kill me, I'd advise you to think about what you've done....Think, and try for some remorse, Riddle," and when Voldemort shuns his suggestion, Harry tries again, "It's all you've got left....I've seen what you'll be otherwise....Be a man...try...Try for some remorse" (*DH*, 741).

When Voldemort makes it clear that he will not heed Harry's suggestions, the two enemies raise their wands and against Voldemort's killing curse, Harry casts his characteristic disarming spell, "*Expelliarmus.*" As Wandinger has observed, Harry avoids using any of the unforgivable curses in this moment, as if implying that his priority is to end a reign of horror, not kill his enemy. Voldemort's death, which results from his own curse rebounding on him, becomes a byproduct but not the intention of Harry's actions.[26] In other words, like Christ, Harry shows compassion towards his enemy.

Harry's sacrifice also facilitates the kind of hope that the Christian story of Jesus depicts: like Jesus' sacrifice, his success ends of a reign of evil. This does not imply that evil has completely disappeared, but rather that the grasp evil once had upon the world will not trump the power of good. This is very much the case in Harry's world—for instance, Draco Malfoy may still hold elitist values, but he might as well be

25   Wandinger, Nikolaus, "'Sacrifice' in *Harry Potter*
26   *Ibid.* from a Girardian Perspective," June 24, 2009, *Innsbrucker Theologischer Leseraum*, http://www.uibk.ac.at/theol/leseraum/texte/819. html.

magically impotent given love's power. It would therefore seem that Harry's sacrifice is very much like the once for all sacrifice the author of Hebrews describes: by voluntarily walking to his death, Harry, like Jesus, brings about a fundamental change in the wizarding world that allows love to permanently defeat evil.

Harry also resembles the scapegoated Christ about which Girard writes. Like Christ, Harry has often been both an object of desire and a scapegoat. As Wandinger, Drexler, and Peter observe, he is both lauded and envied when chosen to participate in the Triwizard Tournament; he is heralded and feared because he can speak Parseltongue.[27] The *Daily Prophet's* portrayal of Harry also shows how the wizarding world could be manipulated to suddenly turn on Harry—one day the public believed Harry was their hero and the next, they considered him the source of all ills. Their opinions were a product of propaganda and denial, because it was easier to blame Harry than to admit the truth of Voldemort's return. Take this exchange between Seamus and Harry as one such example:

"Me mam didn't want me to come back."

"What?" said Harry, pausing in the act of pulling off his robes.

"She didn't want me to come back to Hogwarts."

Seamus turned away from his poster and pulled his own pajamas out of his trunk, still not looking at Harry.

"But—why?" said Harry, astonished. He knew that Seamus's mother was a witch and could not understand, therefore, why she should have come over so Durley-ish.

---

27   Wandinger, Nikolaus, Drexler, Christoph, and Peter, Teresa. 2004. "Harry Potter and the Art of Theology. A Theological Perspective on J. K. Rowling's Novels (Part 2)." *Milltown Studies*, 53, 140-1. Also available from http://www.uibk.ac.at/theol/leseraum/artikel/554.html

Seamus did not answer until he had finished buttoning his pajamas.

"Well," he said in a measured voice, "I suppose… because of you."

"What d'you mean?" said Harry quickly. His heart was beating rather fast. He felt vaguely as though something was closing in on him.

"Well," said Seamus again, still avoiding Harry's eyes, "she…er…well, it's not just you, it's Dumbledore too…"

"She believes the *Daily Prophet*?" said Harry. "She thinks I'm a liar and Dumbledore's an old fool?"

Seamus looked up at him, "Yeah, something like that" (*OP*, 217).

Here we see how even the good guys can fall prey to the *Daily Prophet*'s propaganda because blaming Harry is far safer than admitting the dangers that come with Voldemort. Of course, it is no surprise that Harry's friends are not the only ones who scapegoat to hide that they are jealous or afraid—so are his enemies. In fact, it is easy to read the central conflict between Voldemort and Harry as one in which the villain has scapegoated the protagonist. The prophecy provides one such example of this.

As Rowling emphasizes throughout the series, the prophecy is determinative not because it is truthful in and of itself but because Voldemort *decided* it was truthful and worked for its fulfillment. In Voldemort's mind, only Harry stood between himself and eternal power, which made Harry the enemy, not because he had any special power or ability, but because he was the one Voldemort marked. Here we see the irony of Voldemort's actions: rather than admit his own limitations, Voldemort chose to scapegoat an innocent baby and by so doing, that baby became the one person who could defeat him.

Overall, it seems that two theologies of Christian sacrifice are present in *Harry Potter*: Girard's understanding of sacrifice and Harry's voluntary death as a once for all sacrifice.

But what about Anselm's satisfaction theory? Given that it's historically the most widely accepted view of sacrifice in the Christian tradition, do Rowling's writings touch upon it at all?

The short answer is no, the books don't. The longer answer is that it would be illogical for them to because Anselm's understanding of sin is not Rowling's view of sin. Her characters do not owe a debt to anyone, and there is no sense that Harry's sacrifice is made in order to provide payment to an outside force. This puts Rowling in a curious position: her writings seem to advocate for elements of Christian thought—like the once for all sacrifice—yet other elements of the tradition are left out. In other words, compelling as Girard may be, Anselm's view is the one that has determined a majority of historic Christian thought about sacrifice, and it is not present in the series. This is yet another way in which we see the *Harry Potter* books supporting Christian ideals in a way that blends certain traditional elements with more contemporary principles.

Of course, we cannot forget that Harry's sacrifice is just one of many that characters make in the series. Let's take a look at some others in order to get a fuller view of how the *Harry Potter* series interprets sacrifice.

- **Repeatable Sacrifices**

These sacrifices are so named not because the person in question necessarily repeats them but because their effect is finite, which means that these sacrifices need to happen again and again if their power is to last. We will look at two characters in this section: Lily Potter and Dobby.

Let's think about Lily first. Rowling's explicit use of the sacrificial language undeniably intends Lily to be seen as a sacrificial figure. As Dumbledore tells Harry, "Your mother died to save you...Your mother's sacrifice made the bond of blood the strongest shield I could give you" (*OP*, 736). Indeed, even the images surrounding Lily's death seem to evoke Jesus on the cross. We could conjecture, for instance, that her hands, outstretched to protect her son, allude to the crucifixion itself. Yet there are also several aspects of Lily's sacrifice that prevent a clear parallel with Christ's.

First, Lily's sacrifice was not a once for all sacrifice like Jesus'. The bond of protection that she created for Harry lasted only until he came of age, and after that, he was as vulnerable as the rest of the wizarding world. Also, only Harry was protected by Lily's gift, whereas Jesus' crucifixion and resurrection protected all. This meant that not only did her sacrifice lack permanence, it also did not eradicate the real problem—Voldemort. Following her death, Voldemort was subdued but not defeated; many more sacrifices had to be made to permanently end the violence that affected the wizarding world.

Second, the goal of Lily's sacrifice was different than Christ's: whereas Christ died to save many, Lily had only one concern—her son Harry. As Nikolaus Wandinger, Christoph Drexler, and Teresa Peter remark, "We find no indication that Lily Potter risked and found her death to save Voldemort and his adherents from their evil ways. It was not the love of enemies that motivated her, but a mother's love for her child."[28]

Interestingly, Wandinger, Drexler, and Peter go on to suggest that this difference does not prevent Lily from being a Christ–figure, because both she and Jesus take the violence done to them and transform it into an act of love and salvation.[29] Here I will respectfully nuance what these authors are saying. Though Lily does give her life to save her son, both her motives and the effect of her actions create a parallel that is partial to Jesus' at best. Because her sacrifice did not end Voldemort's reign and because her intentions were not the same as Jesus', there are substantial limitations to relating her sacrifice to Christ's.

So, is it possible to read Lily's sacrifice as a Christian sacrifice? Yes and no. On the no side, we see how it would be harder to argue for a parallel to Christ, as we did with Harry. But on the yes side, Lily gave her life to enact the power of love, and that is certainly in the spirit of Christ. What is also intriguing is the way Lily's sacrifice becomes pivotal to Harry's development: her love protects him, becoming a guiding principle in his life, and he derives the strength to make his own sacrifice because of his mother's love. One even wonders

---

28   *Ibid.* 139.

29   *Ibid.* 136-9.

whether Harry would have grown to be so noble and self-giving without his mother's influence, especially when we consider the way Merope's selfishness seems to have negatively influenced Voldemort's development. So while we might say that Lily's sacrifice is in a different category than Harry's, the way in which her selflessness enables Harry's allows her to participate in the overarching sacrificial framework of the book.

Interestingly, Dobby's sacrifice functions in a very similar way. His death in book seven is without doubt one of the most tragic moments in the entire series, and readers who grew to love Dobby's bulging eyes and earnest loyalty may have felt as much shock as Harry, Hermione, and Ron did at his surprising end.

Dobby died a sacrificial death, knowingly entering the home of his former masters to rescue those trapped at Malfoy Manor. His last moments were ones of glory and pride, because he not only helped his friends but also had a chance to confront his oppressors: "'Dobby has no master!' squealed the elf. 'Dobby is a free elf, and Dobby has come to save Harry Potter and his friends!'" (*DH*, 474).

It seems clear that Dobby's death has similar limitations to Lily's when we ask whether his sacrifice was a Christ-like one. Like Lily's, it is not a once for all sacrifice but rather one that seems to protect Harry for a finite period: it prevents him from dying at Malfoy Manor, and it gives him renewed strength to find the Horcruxes. Also, as with Lily, Dobby's sacrifice was not intended to save the world at large but was rather focused only on his friends—in fact, Dobby made it abundantly clear in the last moments of his life that he has nothing but contempt for his enemies.

But as with Lily's death, I would like to suggest that Dobby's sacrifice ultimately enables Harry's at the end of book seven. As he buries Dobby at Shell Cottage, Harry feels a renewed sense of mission—he knows that he cannot give up on his search to find the Horcruxes because lives like Dobby's depend on it. What we therefore see is that both of these sacrifices formed Harry's personality and shaped him into the kind of person who could give up his life, without objection, so that the entire wizarding community could live in a world that was not dominated by discrimination and violence. In this way, they participate in the only sacrifice in the series that is a true once for all sacrifice.

- **Ambiguous Sacrifices**

The final category of sacrifices I'd like to consider in this chapter are those I will call ambiguous sacrifices, because for one reason or another they do not seem to fully embody the nature of sacrifice. These are particularly intriguing cases because they make us really think about what sacrifice is and what it's not. Let's take a look how Narcissa Malfoy, Cedric Diggory, Sirius Black, Snape, and Dumbledore fit into this category.

We'll begin with Narcissa Malfoy. It may seem counterintuitive to think of Narcissa as someone who is sacrificial—her behavior throughout the novels is haughty and self-righteous, lacking in compassion or generosity. Yet when it comes to her son Draco, Narcissa repeatedly risks her life to protect her son. At the beginning of the sixth book, she endangers herself by asking Snape to make an Unbreakable Vow, knowing that Voldemort could exact vengeance on her for so doing, and in book seven, she lies to Voldemort after he casts the *Avada Kedavra* curse on Harry. Leaning next to Harry under the guise of seeing if he is dead, she asks:

> "*Is Draco alive? Is he in the castle?*"
>
> The whisper was barely audible; her lips were an inch from his ear, her head bent so low that her long hair shielded his face from the onlookers.
>
> "*Yes,*" he breathed back.
>
> He felt the hand on his chest contract; her nails pierced him. Then it was withdrawn. She had sat up.
>
> "He is dead!" Narcissa Malfoy called to the watchers (*DH*, 726).

Narcissa betrays Voldemort because she recognizes that

the only way to rescue her son from Hogwarts is by siding with Harry. She also knows that Voldemort will certainly kill her if her lie is discovered. So do these acts constitute a Christ-like sacrifice? Yes and no. It would seem that Narcissa's selflessness when it comes to her son is much like Lily's, so it would initially appear that one could view both through the same lens. Her lie also helps Harry gain time to find an appropriate opportunity to confront Voldemort, which means that Narcissa—like Lily and Dobby—winds up inadvertently participating in Harry's success.

However, the discerning reader cannot help but feel as if Narcissa's motives were not as pure as Lily or Dobby's. That she loved her son is clear and that she would have given her life for him also seems likely, but overall Narcissa has a limited willingness to make sacrifices for others, and moreover, the people for whom she might make a sacrifice are villainous. She might offer herself for her son and, we might surmise, her husband and sister as well, but these are all people who contribute to violence and oppression.

While we can't say for sure who Lily would give her life for if given the opportunity, we do know that she constantly risked her life for the wizarding world by virtue of being in the Order of the Phoenix. So the difference between Lily's sacrifice and Narcissa's is a qualitative one. If we ask, "Who is Narcissa/Lily making a sacrifice for and what will come of it?" we get radically different answers. These answers help us understand how each character relates to Christ's sacrifice. Were we to ask, "Who did Christ make a sacrifice for and what came of it?" the Christian answer would be, "The whole world and an end to the power of sin, evil and death." If we asked this question of Lily, the answer would be similar—though not the same—as Christ's. With Narcissa, we get a totally different answer: her sacrifices are for family and the continuation of values of exclusion and oppression. To more fully understand the distinction, we might contrast those who made sacrifices for the Nazis and those who made sacrifices for the Underground movement during World War II. Many people made earnest offerings of money, time, or resources to the Nazis because they were committed to the party's cause and wanted that reign of terror to continue.

Were such actions sacrifices? Yes. Did these sacrifices share the same ethics or characteristics as Christ's sacrifice? No. Those who participated in the Underground movement to save Jews and other persecuted groups during World War II also made sacrifices, but with a different spirit—to protect those who were being harmed. Both of these groups made sacrifices but the goals of their offerings could not have been more different. Lily and Narcissa's sacrifices can be read in the same light.

The distinction between Narcissa and Lily therefore points to a fundamental tension in the series: for whom is it worth doing good? Overall, the good characters in the book— like the Weasleys or members of Dumbledore's Army—believe that the entire global family is worth doing good for. Hence, we see Mr. Weasley protecting Muggles, Hermione advocating for house-elves, and students of all ages offering their lives and magical abilities in the Battle of Hogwarts. In contrast, for characters like the Malfoys, the sphere of sacrifice is much smaller, involving only the biological family or Pure-bloods. Because they believe that they are superior human beings, better bred and better wizards, all of their sacrifices, which are sometimes considerable, are tainted by that ideology. So what we learn when we think about Narcissa's sacrifices is that sacrifices must be understood in the context of their environment to know if they truly bear hallmarks of the Christian worldview.

From Narcissa, let us turn to Cedric's death. Can we consider his death at the conclusion of the Triwizard Tournament to be a Christ-like sacrifice? Cedric's is an intriguing case because his death isn't intentional. In contrast with the other characters we've looked at, Cedric doesn't choose to give up something— in this case his life—for the benefit of another. Instead, Cedric dies before he even realizes where he is. So while his death becomes one of the primary reasons Harry is motivated to defeat Voldemort, it is hard to justify his death as similar to Christ's.

Does that mean that his death is in some way senseless? It depends. Insofar as death could be considered an evil, there is something inherently senseless about it. But Harry and other members of Dumbledore's Army make a point of using Cedric's death as a rallying cry: now that Voldemort's hand has touched one of their own, it becomes all the more important to defeat him. In this way, they give his death a purpose and use it as motivation to destroy the power of evil. So while his death may be meaningful, we learn from Cedric that there is a difference between a meaningful death and one that is sacrificial in the way Christ's was.

From here, let us turn to Sirius Black. That he inadvertently disappeared behind a mysterious veil after Bellatrix Lestrange hit him with a curse during a battle at the Ministry of Magic is hardly sacrificial, especially given that he goaded Bellatrix on, literally begging one of the most powerful and dangerous witches to take a shot at him. "Harry saw Sirius duck Bellatrix's jet of red light," Rowling writes. "He was laughing at her. 'Come on, you can do better than that!' he yelled, his voice echoing around the cavernous room" (*OP*, 805).

But if his death is not sacrificial in a standard sense, what about his life? We know that he gave up much for the ideals of love, friendship, and tolerance. He forsook his family to join the Order; he was imprisoned in Azkaban unjustly and forced to live in secrecy following his escape. He protected Harry at the cost of his own freedom at the end of book three, and he must have known when he departed Grimmauld Place for the Ministry that night that he was taking his life in his hands. Such selflessness was at the heart of Sirius's values. His loyalty to the Potters was undying, as was demonstrated by the way Sirius treated his godson: from the moment he escaped Azkaban, Harry was his priority. He tracked him, watching from afar to try to provide whatever protection he could, even if it put him in danger. He makes this philosophy of selflessness explicit at the end of *Prizoner of Azkaban*, when he and Lupin confront the Potters' betrayer, Peter Pettigrew:

> "You don't understand," whined Pettigrew. "He [Voldemort] would have killed me, Sirius!"
>
> "THEN YOU SHOULD HAVE DIED!" roared Black. "DIED RATHER THAN BETRAY YOUR FRIENDS, AS WE WOULD HAVE DONE FOR YOU!" (*PA*, 375).

In many ways, Sirius's comment here embodies the spirit not only of Dumbledore's Army and the Order of the Phoenix—it also embodies the spirit of Christian sacrifice. As is written in John's gospel: "No one has greater love than this, to lay down one's life for one's friends" (15:13).

Sirius displays this characteristic repeatedly, so repeatedly, in fact, that one questions the sincerity of his actions. It is easy to believe that Sirius might have been less motivated by love for his friends and more intrigued by opportunities for danger and adventure. This would mean he was motivated by self-interest rather than selflessness and would, in turn, seriously undermine the possibility of understanding Sirius's sacrifice as Christ-like. And yet, that he loved his friends deeply is also clear. So what kind of verdict can we come to when we consider Sirius? Certain aspects of his life are sacrificial and some are not. Preparation for his death might be, but his actual demise was haphazard and careless. So as we consider Sirius's case, it might be most sensible to say that like Lily and Dobby, his sacrifice may have been flawed but ultimately was undergirded by ideals that align with Christianity.

And now let us consider one of Sirius's least favorite wizards: Severus Snape. Snape is one of the most elusive characters in the series, so it is perhaps no surprise that his relationship to sacrifice is elusive as well. On the one hand, he undertook many sacrificial acts, including working as a double agent to protect Harry and killing Dumbledore so that Draco's soul could remain intact. But on the other hand, we have to ask —as we did with Draco and Narcissa—what is he sacrificing himself for? The reader knows that there is an inherent selfishness to Snape's actions—he was motivated by his self-absorbed devotion to Lily Potter, not by Harry or Dumbledore or the ideals for which they stood. As Dumbledore said to him the night he came to request Snape's help in protecting Lily, "'You disgust me...You do not care, then, about the deaths of her husband and child? They can die, as long as you have what you want?" (*DH*, 677).

What Snape wanted was simple but unattainable, and even in his dying moments, he desired only one thing: Lily's eyes. His character neither changed nor developed in the years since her death, so that he became steadfastly limited by an adoration that consumed him, leaving him jealous, angry, and incapable of loving others. So given his motivations, was Snape truly sacrificing himself for another? No. Noble as his gestures may be, they were not made in the spirit of self-giving love that defines Jesus' sacrifice because Snape was not capable of the kind of love whose primary focus isn't the self but the other.

It is interesting to recognize that Snape did not develop into the adult he turned out to be in a vacuum. Ironically, he is the product of scapegoating by Harry's father, Sirius, and others. It is easy to believe that if he hadn't born the brunt of their bullying, he might have had the opportunity to grow into a kinder, more compassionate man instead of the emotionally limited adult he turned out to be. Here we see an example of Girard's scapegoating mechanism in action, and we notice the way it is an accepted form of violence—how many of us, in reading those passages, grew angry at James Potter or Sirius Black for embarrassing Snape? We thought it was funny or something he deserved for wearing that awful black trenchcoat. Yet reading through Girard's framework, we see how James and Sirius's bullying inflicted lasting harm upon a boy, and that bullying led the child to seek power so that he would never be pushed around again. Hence, Snape's alliance with Voldemort and the development of his dubious personality. In short, much as we may love James and Sirius, is it important to recognize the role they played in making Snape the damaged adult he grew to be.

Finally, we turn to Dumbledore. We know that he asked Snape to kill him in *Half-Blood Prince* in order to prevent the destruction of Draco's soul, so in this way, Dumbledore willingly sacrificed himself for the well-being of another. Heightening the significance of Dumbledore's death is that he died for an enemy's soul, since Draco had more contempt for Dumbledore than most who passed through Hogwarts. Yet we also know that Dumbledore would have died in the near future anyway because of the injury he sustained while searching for Horcruxes. This makes the case of Dumbledore a complicated one: does his sacrifice count if he was going to die anyway?

What is fascinating about Dumbledore is that of all

the characters we have looked at thus far, Dumbledore is one of the few who is evocative of the Anselmian paradigm: he felt responsible for his sister's death, and he spent the rest of his life trying to pay a perceived debt to the ideals he betrayed. After the duel with Grindelwald, which resulted in his Ariana's murder, Dumbledore abandoned his quest for the Deathly Hallows and dominance of the wizarding world and instead dedicated himself to the ideals of acceptance for Muggles and Mudbloods. His commitment to those values eventually pitted him opposite Voldemort and made him loyal to Harry Potter, so that he offered the young wizard all the tools he could think of to facilitate the Dark Lord's defeat.

It is clear that Dumbledore never got over the responsibility he felt for his sister's death and that it haunted him even to the last hours of his life. This is most evident when he cried out while drinking from the torturing Goblet at the end of *Half-Blood Prince*: "'It's all my fault, all my fault,' he sobbed. 'Please make it stop, I know I did wrong, oh please make it stop.'" Several paragraphs later, he adds, "'Don't hurt them, don't hurt them, please, please it's my fault, hurt me instead...'" (572). While the reader can only wager a guess at what images torment the wise old man in that moment, it seems more likely than not that it is that which he most deeply regrets in his life: the death of his sister.

Dumbledore dies as a servant of the ideals that shaped the majority of his life: tolerance, acceptance, forgiveness, and most importantly, love. He also dies refusing to let the ideals that tainted his childhood permanently dominate Draco's. And so his payment is made: his life offered so that another's can be preserved. In so doing, has he made recompense for the evils he perpetrated earlier in the name of oppressive, harmful values? It would seem so, but it would be speculation to presume as much. What can be said more confidently is that his life saved at least one soul from falling prey to Voldemort's destruction.

Tying it all together

What we have just read is a pastiche of the ways that characters' self-offerings do or do not resemble Christ's. It is now time to draw some conclusions about how all these sacrifices relate to one another.

What our investigation showed is that many characters may share certain aspects of Christ's sacrifice, but none is a perfect match. Each has substantial limitations when we look at the motive and accomplishment of these gifts. Yet I would like to suggest, as I did in the Christology chapter, that reading Christ's character and work into the series is not as simple as looking for a single person who fits all the criteria of Jesus. Instead, we find that the net effect of Christ's sacrifices are fulfilled using a variety of characters—without Lily, Harry might not have had the value of sacrifice instilled in him; without Dumbledore, he might not have learned what was worth giving his life for; without Cedric, Sirius, and Dobby, he might not have had the motivation; without Snape and Narcissa, he might have lacked the opportunity, and had Harry not walked to his own death, the wizarding world might never have recovered from Voldemort's reign.

In other words, the identity and work of Christ are alive and vibrant in *Harry Potter*, but they are not represented through a single person. They are brought to life by the contributions of an entire community, as if to say that if the world is going to be dominated by love and tolerance, then the whole world needs to work together towards achieving those ends.

This may be a departure from the typical way in which the Christian story is depicted, but it is my sense that Rowling's writing is not antithetical to it. Christianity teaches that Jesus' sacrifices were made in order to transform the world so that one person at a time people might be converted to the work of inaugurating a kingdom of love and peace. Those who take on that challenge grow to be Christ-*like*, not Christ himself. Read through this lens, we see that the characters in *Harry Potter* function in a similar way. They all accepted the challenge to change their world. None does so perfectly and none does so in isolation, but together, that is what they achieve.

Questions for Your Reflection

1)   Have you found the idea of sacrifice to be unappealing? Why or why not?

2)   Think of the three types of sacrifices (once for all, repeatable, and ambiguous). Which one is the hardest? Do you think it depends on the character? If so, what was the difficulty in each character's sacrifice?

3)   How would Anselem's theory of sin - Jesus dying for a debt that humanity cannot pay itself – be possible for the Harry Potter series? What would need to be added?

4)   It seems like certain characters orient themselves in a way that invites sacrifice. Cedric's heroism and bravery along with Narcissa's love for Draco are examples of this. Is this trait present in other characters? How does one shape their orientation this way?

5)   One of my students once said that the Ministry of Magic scapegoated Mudbloods and Muggles in book seven. What are other examples of the way that the Ministry scapegoats in the series?

CHAPTER 6:

Flesh of the Servant Willingly Given

The Eucharist

Theological Meals

I TOOK A LECTURE with Dean Laura King my senior year at Yale because it was the only English course that fit into my schedule. Dean King, as we called her, was a small woman with dark brown hair who, to my memory, wore nothing but black. She'd grown up in various parts of Asia, adopted Buddhism, and worked as a journalist in the States before becoming a professor. She taught a creative writing course that drew nearly one hundred students each term as well as a course on medieval drama, which draw a small number of upper class English majors. I took the latter.

The class was typical in that it was divided into two parts—weekly lectures and a discussion. But that was pretty much the only structural similarity Medieval English Drama had with other courses. Dean King took charge of our discussion sections, which are customarily the turf of teaching assistants. She also held the sections in her on-campus apartment instead of a classroom, in the evening instead of during the day, and every time we met together, she baked.

It started at our first discussion, when Dean King asked a question and there was the awkward silence typical of most college classes (this phenomenon occurs when no one wants to take the plunge, no one wants to make a mistake, or--heaven forbid--no one does the reading). After a few minutes of quiet, Dean King said, "That's it. You need help," and she came back with an unopened box of Trader Joe's vanilla meringues. After that, we talked.

Every meeting thereafter my professor laid out treats on her coffee table ranging from homemade cupcakes, to biscotti, or ice cream. When I asked Dean King why she had treats prepared for us each week, she said, "Sugar makes students' brains work." I don't know if this is true or not, but I do know that with each batch of cookies or popcorn balls that Dean King prepared for us, members of our class not only became more involved in discussions; we also began to love medieval English drama. Reading morality plays became a pleasure rather than a chore, and many of us said that going to section was our favorite part of the week. We began to meet outside of class, setting up times to read plays together or study.

At the final exam—to which Dean King brought a tub of freshly baked brownies—I was genuinely sad. I felt nostalgia for our weekly discussions, the learning and laughter that went on as talked about a dramatic rewrite of Noah's ark or how the play *Gallathea* might have influenced Shakespeare's *Twelfth Night*. I wasn't likely to have an experience like that again because our discussion sections weren't just an hour in which we discussed a given set of topics. Our weekly meals had made class a community, and that was something really special to college students like us, who were far from home and far from anyone who cared enough about us to bake on a regular basis.

Dean King left Yale shortly after our class. She left no forwarding address, and to my knowledge, no one in New Haven knows her whereabouts. I like to believe that she knows the impact she's made on her students, and I also like to think that she's living in Tibet and writing stories, because she often said that was her dream.

I now bake for my students each week. Sadly, I'm not the baker Laura King was. I fear that my culinary adventures bear results like unto Hagrid's—I tried making sugar cookies out of roll-out dough and managed to make rock cakes instead—but my students never complain, so I can't be sure. They think that they're getting a treat, but I know the real power of rice krispie treats and every flavor cupcakes lies not in the taste but in the sharing. Meals form community, as any family that eats together each night, any member of Dean King's seminar, or any Christian can tell you.

The Eucharist, or the Lord's Supper, is the Christian meal. It is also one of the most distinctive parts of the Christian worship service and one of the most complicated. Every denomination has its own understanding of what the Eucharist is and what it accomplishes. Since these beliefs are too numerous and complicated to discuss in detail, we will be looking at the history of the Eucharist and some of the most prominent interpretations of it. We will then see how Rowling makes explicit use of Eucharistic imagery in *Harry Potter and the Goblet of Fire.*

A Brief History of the Eucharist

The origins of the Christian Eucharist are surprisingly not in the gospels but the Book of Exodus. This early biblical book tells the story of the Jewish people's four hundred-year long slavery in Egypt and how God rescued them from their bondage. God did this by telling Moses to issue a commandment to the Jewish people: they were to find an unblemished, one-year-old male lamb, one for every house, and if each house couldn't afford a lamb, they were to join together with another household to get one. At the appointed time, each family would take its lamb, slaughter it, and put its blood on their doors. Following that, they were to roast the lamb and eat it with unleavened bread and bitter herbs—the bread had to be unleavened because this was an urgent meal, and there wouldn't be enough time for it to rise. Because the meal was so rushed, the people were also instructed to eat as if they were walking out the door—with staff in hand, already clothed and with sandals on their feet.

The Jewish people were able to protect themselves from the massacre that followed the Passover by taking these steps, for God said that following the meal:

I will pass through the land of Egypt that night, and I will strike down every firstborn in the land of Egypt, both human beings and animals; on all the gods of Egypt I will execute judgments: I am the LORD. The blood shall be a sign for you on the houses where you live: when I see the blood, I will pass over you, and no plague shall destroy you when I strike the land of Egypt (Ex. 12:12-13).

This mass slaughter finally convinced the Egyptian Pharaoh to release the Jewish people, albeit with a brief change of heart as they approached the Red Sea. That event became pivotal in Jewish history because by assuring their liberation, God kept the promises of the covenant: the Israelites are set free to wander through the wilderness of Sinai and reach the promised land.

In thanksgiving for God's deliverance, the Book of Exodus instructs the Jewish people to commemorate this Passover on a yearly basis. The holiday lasts seven to eight days, depending on whether you live inside or outside of Israel, and during it, Jewish people recreate the night that God protected them by eating unleavened bread, lamb, and bitter herbs (wine is also an essential part of the ceremony). This commemoration is known as a *seder*, and *seders* are usually held once or twice during the Passover holiday.

We know that Jesus participated in the Passover *seder* in his own day, and his celebration of it is recorded in the synoptic gospels—Matthew, Mark, and Luke. These texts say that Jesus celebrated the *seder* with unleavened bread and, we can only assume, with lamb and bitter herbs. But what is interesting about the record we have of that Passover, which Christians call the Last Supper, is the way in which it differed from the traditional Jewish *seder*. Observe Luke's account below:

When the hour came, he took his place at the table, and the apostles with him. He said to them, "I have eagerly desired to eat this Passover with you before I suffer; for I tell you, I will not eat it until it is fulfilled in the kingdom of God." Then he took a cup, and after giving thanks he said, "Take this and divide it among yourselves; for I tell you that from now on I will not drink of the fruit of the vine until the kingdom of God comes." Then he took a loaf of bread and when he had given thanks, he broke it and gave it to them saying, "This is my body, which is given for you. Do this in remembrance of me." And he did the same with the cup after supper, saying, "This cup that is poured out for you is the new covenant of my blood." (Lk. 22:14-20).

In the Jewish *seder*, there is no suggestion that the bread and wine are intended to represent body and blood. So what Jesus did was to take that traditional ceremony and put a twist on it: the bread and wine of the *seder* were given a new meaning outside of the Exodus story. They were to be associated with the sacrifice Jesus was about to make. What this symbolizes is that if the Passover lamb was sacrificed to save the Jewish people from bondage, Jesus was to be the new lamb slaughtered to save people from a different type of bondage: sin. Many Christians commemorate the idea of Jesus as metaphoric lamb at their Eucharistic services, when they recite an ancient prayer called the *Agnus Dei*, saying, "Lamb of God, you take away the sins of the world. Have mercy on us."

Finally, Jesus gives explicit instructions to the disciples about the repetition of this Eucharistic ceremony: "Do this in remembrance of me," he says (Lk. 22:19). In Greek, this is called the *anamnesis*, or the remembrance that charges the disciples and future Christians to commemorate Jesus' salvific work by recreating this meal.

A Brief Aside about John

There is no Eucharistic celebration in John; instead, the story is replaced with the footwashing ceremony where Jesus washes the feet of his disciples. Yet interestingly, the writer still explicitly shows that Jesus is the new Passover Lamb. This is because in John's gospel, Jesus dies not during the Passover, as he does in the other three gospels, but before it, on the day of Preparation, when the Jewish people would have been slaughtering their own lambs for the holiday. By changing the date on which Jesus dies, John suggests that Jesus offered himself as a replacement for the lamb used by the Jewish people, giving himself to save the world from the bondage of sin, just as the lamb was sacrificed to save the Jewish people from the bondage of slavery. As a result, it would be impossible for Jesus to celebrate the Last Supper in John's gospel because he would have already died and risen again.

So what do Christians do today?

The celebration of the Eucharist is central within most Christian denominations, but Christian groups tend to have widely divergent interpretations of the meal, and because there are so many Christian denominations, it would be impossible to catalogue all the nuances of their beliefs.

That said, Christians also share many common beliefs about what the Eucharist does and what it accomplishes. So rather than focuses on the differences between Christian denominations, let's concentrate for a moment on what they all share:

The Eucharist is a commemoration, not a second sacrifice. Christians believe that the sacrifice Jesus made is a once-for-all sacrifice, so powerful that it does not need to be repeated or redone. As it says in the Letter to the Hebrews, "For by a single offering he has perfected for all time those who are sanctified. And the Holy Spirit also testifies to us, for after saying, 'This is the covenant that I will make with them after those days, says the Lord: I will put my laws in their hearts, and I will write them on their mind,' he also adds, 'I will remember their sins and their lawless deeds no more.' Where there is forgiveness of these, there is no longer any offering for sin" (10:14-18).

The Eucharist foreshadows and Christians remember. Because the Last Supper foreshadowed Jesus' death, Christians use the Eucharistic celebration as a memory of Jesus' sacrifice for them. In this way, the Eucharist is an act of remembering that keeps the Christian story alive.

Jesus is saying, "I am life."   By partaking of the Eucharist, Christians believe that they attain fullness of life on earth and in Heaven. This belief is rooted biblical texts like that of the Gospel of John, where Jesus says, "I am the bread of life" (6:48).

Jesus is saying, "I am that which unites." Christians believe that by sharing the same bread and the same cup, they are united as one collective body. In this way, the Eucharist is fundamentally an act that builds community. This belief is rooted in Paul's First Letter to the Corinthians, where he writes, "The cup of blessing that we bless, is it not a sharing in the blood of Christ? The bread that we break, is it not a sharing in the body of Christ? Because there is one bread, we who are many are one body, for we all partake of the one bread" (10:16-17).

Jesus is saying, "I am abundance and bread for the journey." Christians believe that when they eat a small piece of bread and take a sip of wine or grape juice each week, their souls are deeply nourished, and they become what they celebrate. In response, Christians also believe that they must nourish and transform the world just as they have been nourished and transformed after receiving the bread and wine. That means that the Eucharist also has ethical implications: Christians are not only receiving bread for themselves. They must become like the bread—a source through which God can deliver grace and love—in their relationships with others.

A mystery of faith (*mysterium fidei*). Christians believe that the Eucharist is an essential part of what Jesus did to save humans from sin. But though they recognize something of the Eucharist's significance, they simultaneously believe that their understanding will never be complete. As a result, many denominations recognize that there is something mysterious about the Eucharist, and they vocalize this in their prayers. The Latin phrase *mysterium fidei*—which translated means the mystery of faith—is the theological term that Christians use to express this sense of the unfathomable. Often they recite these words in a prayer they say each time the Eucharist is celebrated, "Therefore we proclaim the mystery of faith: Christ has died, Christ is risen, Christ will come again."

These characteristics illustrate that Christians believe that the Eucharist is not just a historic event; it is an act that continually transforms people and their relationship to God. So how does Rowling make use of the Eucharist in the *Harry Potter* series? In a surprising way, as we shall see in a moment!

An Anti-Eucharist for the Anti-Christ

As we saw in the chapter on Christology, J.K. Rowling creates a Jesus-figure for the series who is found in a community of many people rather than one. Because of that, it would initially seem as if a Eucharistic celebration would be impossible in the books—after all, who would be responsible for celebrating it?

Indeed a casual read through the books shows that there is no equivalent of the Last Supper...at least not in the traditional sense. What I will suggest here is that J.K. Rowling takes the Christian Eucharist and turns it on its head in order to show the depths of evil and the power of good; by so doing, she promotes the Christian message in a new and somewhat unconventional way.

To understand this theme in *Harry Potter*, we need to refer back to the end of *Goblet of Fire*. Harry and Cedric have just touched the Triwizard Cup and been transported to the cemetery in Little Hangleton, where they are greeted by Wormtail, who kills Cedric and binds Harry. Wormtail then proceeds with a ritual, excerpted below, that restores Voldemort to bodily form:

> And now Wormtail was whimpering. He pulled a long, thin, shining silver dagger from inside his cloak. His voice broke into petrified sobs.
>
> *"Flesh—of the servant—w-willingly given—you will— revive—your master."*
>
> He stretched his right hand out in front of him—the hand with the missing finger. He gripped the dagger very tightly in his left hand and swung it upward.
>
> Harry realized what Wormtail was about to do a

second before it happened—he closed his eyes as tightly as he could, but he could not block the scream that pierced the night, that went through Harry as though he had been stabbed with the dagger too. He heard something fall to the ground, heard Wormtail's anguished panting, then a sickening splash, as something was dropped into the cauldron. Harry couldn't stand to look…but the potion had turned a burning red; the light of it shone through Harry's closed eyelids…

Wormtail was gasping and moaning with agony. Not until Harry felt Wormtail's anguished breath on his face did he realize that Wormtail was right in front of him.

"B-blood of the enemy…forcibly taken…you will… resurrect your foe" (GOF, 641-2).

This quotation shows something I will call an Anti-Eucharist, meaning that this ritual is the opposite of what a Eucharist is supposed to be for several reasons:

Direct Allusion to the Biblical Text: This passage from *Goblet of Fire* alludes to the biblical depictions of the Last Supper, but with a twist. In the Bible, Jesus says, "This is my body, which is given for you" and later, "This cup that is poured out for you is the new covenant of my blood" (Lk. 22:19-20). Wormtail also uses language about sacrificial body and blood, but it is not given freely, as Jesus' is. Harry's blood is "forcibly taken," while Wormtail's body is subjected to great physical agony. One might also conjecture that Wormtail's supposedly "willingly given" flesh is offered under threat of death or torture (*GOF*, 641-2).

Self-interest and Suffering: There is something inherently selfish in what Voldemort is doing: he experiences no pain during his bodily resurrection but demands that Wormtail and Harry give their of their own flesh and blood. In contrast, Christians believe that the Eucharistic celebration commemorates the selflessness of Jesus, who felt pain so that others were spared.

One for Many vs. Many for One: In the Christian Eucharist, the faithful remember that Jesus gave himself for the salvation of the whole world—that means that one person sacrificed for the good of many. This is the opposite of what we see in Rowling's depiction: instead of the self-offering of one person, we see several people—such as Harry and Wormtail—sacrificing themselves for a single individual: Voldemort. Put differently, while Jesus' body and blood is bread and drink offered the resurrection of the whole world, Voldemort is the sole consumer of the meal given by Harry and Wormtail.

Offering of Good vs. Offering of Evil: Finally, and perhaps most importantly, the Eucharistic celebration and the Anti-Eucharist in *Goblet of Fire* achieve radically different ends. The Eucharistic celebration is considered by Christians to be just that, a celebration of the gift Jesus gave to humanity to ensure its wholeness and resurrection. In contrast, Voldemort's resurrection is at heart an evil that does not lead to fulfillment but rather to the torture and death of many innocent wizards and Muggles.

In light of these contrasts, it seems clear that Rowling wrote this passage in *Goblet of Fire* with the Christian Eucharistic celebration in mind. But why would she do this? It would seem that she is trying to turn the Christian Eucharist on its head, and my understanding is that she did so for a very specific reason: to illuminate the depths of Voldemort's maleficence and, in turn, the Savior's goodness. In other words, she is setting up an anti-hero, literally a Christ-opposite or Anti-Christ. This Anti-Christ shows by counter-example what it means to be a savior, always doing the opposite of what is good, the opposite of what is salvific. Writing an Anti-Eucharist in which the Anti-Christ Voldemort clearly manipulates Christian themes in an un-Christian way allows Rowling to drive this point home. Likewise, the Anti-Eucharist gives Rowling a vehicle to point to the real Eucharist by saying, "Look, what Voldemort is doing is clearly wrong. A true savior would never do something like this." Hence, by showing the opposite of what is good, Rowling illuminates the model itself; by showing what is evil, the reader is led towards what is good.

I can imagine that some readers may wonder if toying with the Eucharist in this way is heretical. In response to this objection, I would like to suggest that Rowling's decision to turn the Eucharist upside down and fashion Voldemort into an Anti-Christ does illuminate the Christian message, but it does so in an unconventional way. Most writers who want to communicate the Good News of the faith write using allegory so that the Christian message is clear and vibrant, unmissable to the reader. C.S. Lewis's *The Lion, the Witch, and the Wardrobe* is perhaps the most prominent modern example of such writing. The benefit of writing in this way is that the reader cannot overlook Christianity's presence in the novel: Aslan is clearly Jesus; Edmund is clearly Peter, etc. The downside is that it lacks subtlety. Books like *The Lion, the Witch, and the Wardrobe* scream out Christianity's tenets to even the nonchalant reader, and they may turn off readers who dislike dogma or the feeling that they are being preached at.

In contrast, Rowling chooses to avoid allegory and depicts Christian themes in more poetic ways—by writing an Anti-Eucharist or depicting the person of Christ as an entire community, as we saw in the previous chapter. Her method is therefore both more subtle and unconventional than that of many other writers who touch upon Christian themes in their novels. The benefit—what stays in the suitcase—is that Rowling's writing may appeal more to non-Christians or to those wary of dogma because it allows the reader to see the truths of Christianity through a new lens. The downside is that it leaves others questioning whether the books are Christian in orientation.

Cleaning up after dinner

If my students learn something about the Eucharist in class, I hope it occurs not only through the readings but also through the desserts we share together. Of course, these are not Eucharistic feasts, but they bear some simple similarities: they build community, they create memories, and they provide a sense of comfort. They allow my students to see the power of a meal, and maybe by doing that, each of them gets a glimpse of what the Eucharist is like.

Questions for Your Reflection

1)   What are your thoughts on the anti-Eucharist? Are there any other examples in the series of Christian themes being inverted for the sake of revealing that theme's power?

2)   The Eucharist is a site of remembrance. What other things in the wizarding world take remembrance to have power?

3)   Fellowship is an important component of the Eucharist. How does fellowship come about in the anti-Eucharist? How is fellowship celebrated among the good guys even without specifically Eucharistic imagery?

4)   Readers might be unaware of the Eucharist scene of sorts in *The Goblet of Fire*. Does their lack of knowledge keep them from fully understanding the significance of that scene in the series? Similarly, does the Eucharist in Christian liturgy require knowledge of its meaning to be experienced well? Why or why not?

5)   What do you think of the subtlety of J.K. Rowling as opposed to the obvious presence of Christianity that C.S. Lewis infuses into *The Chronicles of Narnia*? What do you find to be the strengths and weaknesses of each?

CHAPTER 7:

Try for a Little Remorse

Salvation

Saving the Wizarding World, Saving our World

O NE OF MY STUDENTS approached me before our class on salvation. He was an eloquent young man with a light sense of humor and affable demeanor. He spoke often in class, with an earnestness that I admired, and he always took the comments of other students to heart. On that day, he approached me with a bit of trepidation and then a grin. "I'm going to be baptized," he said.

I smiled back at him and couldn't help myself. "Did our class finally get to you?" I laughed.

"No," he said, "but Jesus did. I was saved."

Though mildly disappointed that he wouldn't walk around for the rest of his life talking about the profound effect our seminar had on his spiritual development, I was moved by my student's choice to make a commitment to something he believed—that he had been saved.

The language of salvation has been one of the most characteristic features of Christianity since the beginning of the religion, and Christians certainly have a monopoly on the idea that people can be 'saved.' But what does that phrase actually mean? For Christians, salvation has two components. The first part is recognizing that there is a problem that affects all humans—sin. The second is a solution that corrects that flaw, and that solution results in salvation. But as we saw in the chapter on sin, Christians have several ways of understanding what the problem is, and so it should come as no surprise that the solution—salvation—is explained in many ways as well.

The end of the *Harry Potter* series also has a solution to its conflict—the biggest problem for characters that once worried about surviving deadly curses now seems to be whether or not their children will get along at school. But just because the story has a happy ending doesn't mean that there's anything like salvation present. If we want to know if any of the characters in J.K. Rowling's saga experience something like salvation, we need to know what Christians think about it. So without wasting another second, let's dig in and see what salvation looks like for Christians, for Harry Potter, and for the wizarding world!

Six Ways Jesus Saves

What do Christians mean when they talk about salvation? Depending on the denomination and the time period, Christians have thought, and continue to think, in a variety of ways about salvation. As we will see, a lot of the variation has to do with the root of the problem—sin. We saw in the sin chapter that Christians have several vocabularies for understanding sin's power, and that means that salvation can be explained in different ways as well. Of course, the punishment must fit the crime—or in this case, the clemency must fit the sin! So for instance, if sin is defined as willful personal disobedience, a description of salvation as Jesus' defeat over the cosmic forces of evil does little to solve the problem.

In his article, "Six Ways of Salvation," Ted Peters looks at six frameworks Christians use to explain what it means to be saved. Let's take a brief look at these and see how they relate to other topics we've already discussed:

Jesus as Teacher of True Knowledge: This idea is one of two that can be traced back to Peter Abelard, a medieval theologian who was a student of Anselm's and who lived from 1079-1142. Abelard suggested that humanity's problem is ignorance and that ignorance resulted in sin; put differently, humans don't know how to live ethical, wholesome lives, and they fail to do so because of that. Since the problem is ignorance, the solution is an incredibly good teacher, which Abelard called a moral exemplar. Unfortunately, humans aren't in a position to be moral exemplars themselves because, tainted by sin, they lack enough knowledge to act wisely and virtuously. Abelard said that only Jesus was in a position to be the example that humans needed. In the Jesus as Teacher of True Knowledge model, Jesus brings salvation by teaching humans about God and their souls. Because humans live in the darkness of their ignorance, Jesus lights the way by giving information about who God is and how to live in right relationship with the Divine. Biblical stories of the Sermon on the Mount and the parables Jesus told are examples of the way Jesus communicated knowledge to humans. The choices he made also serve as an ethical guide for people on their life journeys.

Jesus as Moral Example and Influence: This is the second of the frameworks that comes from Abelard. In this conception, the problem for humans is slightly different: instead of being unable to gain knowledge, humans are unable to love well. This doesn't mean that they can't love at all; it means that they love improperly. As Ted Peters writes, "We love naturally, of course; but we love ourselves and those in our families or business partners who can reciprocate love. We love when it profits us." We saw something of this in Narcissa Malfoy's behavior, as we discussed in the chapter on sacrifice. Narcissa loved only those for whom it was convenient, people like Draco and other Pure-bloods. Peters continues, "In shocking contrast, by example Jesus teaches us to love the other as other, to love outsiders and even enemies."[30] Because this is not a natural inclination for humans, Jesus leads by example, living a life rooted in love of God and the world at large. When humans follow that example and commit to love the way Jesus loves—caring for all people and not just those for whom it is convenient—they help to bring about the reign of peace God

---

30   Peters, Ted. "Six Ways of Salvation: How Does Jesus Save?" *Dialog*. 45:3. Fall 2006. 226.

hopes to create on earth.

Jesus as Victorious Champion and Liberator: This model has two parts. Swedish theologian Gustaf Aulén advocated for the Victorious Champion framework. Aulén believed that evil was the primary problem humans encountered, and so from Aulén's perspective, Jesus literally engages in a battle against evil, the devil, and sin when he dies. His victory is witnessed in the resurrection, making Jesus a triumphant battle warrior who defeated death by rising again, as if to say, "Ha, Death! You think you have power!" Salvation in this framework means that humans are no longer subject to the bondage of evil. The Liberator framework derives from the work of liberation theologians. Liberation theology began with a group of thinkers in twentieth-century Latin America in who saw humanity's problem in terms of human oppression. They read the biblical narrative as a story of domination ranging from Egyptian oppression of the Israelites to psychological oppression by sin. Jesus offered salvation to humans by uncovering these structures and providing solidarity and hope in suffering. In this framework, when people work to alleviate oppression, they participate in the goal that God has for humanity: to create a world motivated by peace and justice, not persecution or subjection.

Jesus as our Satisfaction: We've already covered this theory in the chapter on sacrifice, but as a quick reminder, satisfaction theory originated with Anselm of Canterbury. Anselm said that humanity's sins resulted in an unpayable debt to God that had to be paid to preserve God's justice. Jesus was the only person in a position to make recompense to God because of his unique fully-God-and-fully-human identity. Jesus provided salvation by paying the debt to the divine.

Jesus as Happy Exchange: We read in the Christology chapter about how Christians think that Jesus is both fully God and fully human. In the Happy Exchange model, humans receive salvation because they can incorporate attributes of the divine into their own faith. That creates the possibility to exchange sinful human attributes for faithful ones.

Jesus as the Final Scapegoat: This topic came up in

our discussion of René Girard in the sacrifice chapter. Girard suggested that humanity's primary problem was the way it used scapegoating to get off the hook for wrongdoings. Jesus uncovered the inappropriateness of the scapegoating cycle. When Jesus became a scapegoat, his death revealed just how unacceptable this practice was. As Ted Peters writes, "In principle, Jesus is the final scapegoat, because the lie no longer can fool us into believing we can justify ourselves by sacrificing others."[31] In this model, salvation is rendered when humans find new and healthier ways to be in relationship to God— through faith in God and love of neighbor.

Looking at this list, it might seem as if Christians think anything and everything about salvation. Is that a problem— does it mean Christians don't really *know* what they think about salvation? The short answer is no. In many ways, these six frameworks use different vocabulary to express the same thing: humanity has a fundamental source of suffering, something that keeps each person from living a whole and fulfilling life. Sometimes this is because people make poor choices, and sometimes it is because people are victims of other people's poor choices. On the cross and in the resurrection, Jesus takes steps to address this problem, whatever form it takes, and gives humanity tools to make their lives more completely one with God. On these fundamental principles, Christians agree. The different theories about what happens in salvation are therefore useful because they give people words to express Jesus' salvific work that resonate with their own situations.

Another way to think about this is to think about what it's like when you experience something really strong or overwhelming, like the first time you fell in love or when you experienced the death of someone you cared about.

Those moments are overpowering, so overpowering that it's often hard to find words to express them to others. As time passes, the significance of that event grows more defined in your memory, and you're able to vocalize it in new ways, so that the truth of the event remains the same, but your descriptions

---

31   *Ibid.* 234.

Chart of the Six Ways Jesus Saves Adapted from Ted Peters

Model	Human Problem	What Jesus Does	How Humans Respond
Teacher	Lack of knowledge	Teach Knowledge	Humans learn and follow the way
Moral Example	Lack of knowledge about love	Teach God's love and liberation	Copy Jesus and live ethically
Victorious Champion	Bondage to Evil	Liberation from bondage	Accept God's grace
Satisfaction	Sin & Loss of Blessedness	Satisfaction of Cosmic Justice	Accept God's Grace
Happy Exchange	Sin & Loss of Blessedness	Exchange of Attributes	Exchange of Attributes
Final Scapegoat	Self-Justification and Scapegoating	Revelation of Human Self-Justification and Scapegoating	Realization of Scapegoating and God's Justification

might take different forms. Salvation is something like this. It is something elusive and intense that needs many different images and symbols to fully express its depth and importance. The biblical writers recognized this too because they employed a number of different images and symbols to help capture what salvation was all about. In turn, theological writers tapped into these different representations when they wrote the theories we just discussed. Hence, there is truth in each one, but, as Ted Peters says at the closing of his article, "None can claim a copyright for exclusive rights on what the Bible says."[32] There is truth in all these frameworks and that the same truth can be explained in so many different ways is perhaps the beauty at the core of this Christian belief.

Salvation in *Harry Potter*

If sin, evil, and death are the issues Jesus counters in the cross and resurrection, what needs to be saved in the wizarding world? What is the problem that needs to be redressed, and are those problems and solutions similar to the ones Jesus addresses?

As postulated in the chapter on sin, there are two overarching crises in the wizarding world: intolerance and lack of community. These two are interrelated—there is no united community because some wizards have no respect for others and vice versa. As we will see, *Harry Potter* taps into four of the above paradigms to address these problems; however, as we've said before, the series uses many characters—not just a single God-Man—as vehicles to redress these ailments. Let's take a look at a few such characters and how they fit into the frameworks above:

1. **Dumbledore as Teacher of Knowledge**: More than any other witch or wizard, including Hermione, Dumbledore gave Harry the information he needed to defeat Voldemort. He told him about the power of love in earlier books, exposed him to Voldemort's biography in the sixth, and even in the last pages of book seven, it is Dumbledore

---

32   *Ibid.* 235.

in King's Cross who clarifies the secrets of the Horcruxes and Hallows. In fact, Dumbledore is so intelligent that he is even able to anticipate what knowledge his students will need in the future, as when he bequeaths the Tales of Beedle the Bard to Hermione, the Deluminator to Ron, and the old snitch to Harry. In all these ways, the Harry Potter books impress upon us that Dumbledore is the smartest and wisest wizard in the Harry's world.

What makes Dumbledore fit into the Teacher of Knowledge category is not just his intelligence but the way he uses it to end intolerance and lack of community in the wizarding world. He works tirelessly to teach the wizards about the dangers of intolerance—especially in his work as headmaster of Hogwarts—and he also serves as a well-known advocate for Mudbloods and Muggles. In this way, we can see the way in which Dumbledore parallels Jesus as teacher of knowledge. Like Jesus, Dumbledore provides a practical ethical framework for wizards, a way that will lead to peace and harmony if they follow it diligently.

2. **Lily as the Moral Exemplar:** Jesus as Moral Exemplar is the supreme teacher of love for Christians, and throughout the Harry Potter series, Lily Potter is understood to be the person, above all others, who teaches Harry how to love. In fact, her love is so deep and abiding that it not only provides powerful protection, it also gives Harry a path to follow. To be as loving and giving as his mother is something Harry learns over time and which comes to fruition at the end of book seven, when it's Harry's turn to imitate his mother and offer his life out of love for others. As he tells Voldemort in their last duel together, "I was ready to die to stop you from hurting these people...I've done what my mother did. They're protected from you. Haven't you noticed how none of the spells you put on them are binding? You can't torture them. You can't touch them" (DH, 738). By the end of the series, we see how Harry's love protects others, just as Lily's love protected him. Harry has grown into the image of his mother, finally able to follow her example and give his love in a

profound, intense and selfless way.

3. **Dumbledore's Army as Victorious Champions:** The Victorious Champion model had two parts to it: Jesus as one who defeats evil and Jesus as liberator. Let's begin with the first part. The *Harry Potter* series is a cosmic battle between good and evil. Though that battle is played out quite literally in book seven, it provides the overarching theme for the entire series, forcing every character to participate by taking the side of the good, the evil, or occasionally, the cowardly (enter Gilderoy Lockhart). While many characters wage war against the powers of evil, I would like to highlight three of them here. First, Harry. Because Harry is the one who literally defeats evil in battle—aka Voldemort—he is the most obvious parallel to Aulén's victorious Christ. Yet because Voldemort's soul has been fractured, the actual killing of Voldemort is really just the last piece in a complex puzzle. This brings us to the other two characters I'd like to discuss: Ron Weasley and Neville Longbottom. By destroying the locket and killing Nagini, Ron and Neville participate in the defeat of evil by dispelling two other powerful agents of evil, Horcruxes. Without their efforts, the reader can easily see how the battle at Hogwarts could have been lost, or worse yet, never happened. But what is perhaps even more interesting is the way in which Ron and Neville's victories allow them to defeat their own inner demons. In Neville's case, that meant overcoming insecurities to become a confident leader. He was already well towards that goal by the time he destroyed the giant snake, but we might understand Nagini's death as the moment when he truly comes into his own. He receives Gryffindor's sword—which in and of itself is a vote of confidence in his leadership skills—and rallies the forces at Hogwarts even when he believes Harry to be dead. Ron's trajectory also shows an internal victory over evil: Ron literally speaks to his own inner demons when he destroys the Horcrux, as if he has been given the opportunity to tell his own insecurities that they deserve to be in the grave. His story

shows the psychological or interior component to evil, that evil may be a powerful force inside the individual as well as in the outside world. Both must be overcome for evil to truly be defeated. The second part of the Victorious Champion model had to do with Jesus as liberator of the oppressed. While several characters are liberators in the series—like Dumbledore and Mr. Weasley—one stands out above the others: Hermione Granger. From an early age, Hermione worked tirelessly to grant freedoms to those who were denied. She spent hours in the library looking for legal loopholes to free Buckbeak, and she formed the unpopular organization S.P.E.W.—the Society for the Promotion of Elfish Welfare—to end the bondage of the house-elves. She has a passion for equality and a prophetic voice that speaks up even when it is unpopular. Just as Jesus ate with tax collectors, prostitutes, and sinners—the Mudbloods and house-elves of his era— so Hermione never ceased to do what is right simply because it was unaccepted. Instead, she became a model of someone who speaks out about oppression and works for the liberation of those whom society systematically harms.

4. **Harry as the Final Scapegoat:** We've already discussed Harry's role as a scapegoat at length in the chapter on sacrifice, so I won't say much about it here, but what is worth reiterating is that Harry's sacrifice, like Jesus', permanently ends the validity of scapegoating, and by so doing, Voldemort's worldview no longer holds sway for wizards. Even if remnants of it persist after Harry's salvific actions, people can no longer perpetrate violations that once went unquestioned. In other words, the wizarding world is no longer blind to the injustice of prejudice and intolerance.

And that takes us full circle: each of these four frameworks contributes to salvation for the wizarding world because they effectively end the power of intolerance and inaugurate a stronger community. But none of these characters achieves this goal alone. Unlike the Christian story, where one individual procures salvation for the world, it is the work of every member of Dumbledore's Army in *Harry Potter*. This is a wonderfully symbolic move on Rowling's part: she uses the solution to solve the problem. If the problems are intolerance and a lack of community, then the members of Dumbledore's Army create a united community to fight against discrimination and inaugurate a reign of peace.

Salvation and Community

One might argue that the communal aspect of salvation in the novels undermines Christian principles. At a literal level, this may be the case—the New Testament narratives certainly place the burden of salvation on one individual. Yet even Jesus didn't act in isolation—together with the guidance of the creator God (God the Father) and with the sustenance of God the Holy Spirit, Jesus undertook his mission. Without the love of his mother, Mary, he might not have been born; without the formation of his earthly teachers, he might not have become a rabbi and without faithful witnesses, Christians might not have a record of his life. The work of Jesus may be unique, but it was without doubt accomplished in the community of the Trinity and the earthly world. Likewise, salvation for the wizarding world was enacted in a communal setting. Wizards and witches had to work together, under the guidance of love, in order to triumph over Voldemort.

When we get to this moment in class, I hope that this point sticks with my students. In the mindset of Christianity and *Harry Potter*, creating a just, loving, and vibrant world may be primarily the work of one being, but it can only become a reality with the support of others. In the Christian worldview, this community is known as the Church. Together members of the Church work to bring Jesus' ideals into the world by worshipping together, remembering Jesus' stories, and doing social justice work. By opening themselves up to doing God's work on earth, they become what is known as the body of Christ.

For my student who was baptized as a member of the church over a year ago, he chose to make that commitment explicit in a profound way. But I also see my students doing the work of the Church regardless of whether they attend weekly services or even profess themselves to be Christian. Many of them volunteer in the economically impoverished areas of New Haven; one of my students teaches English to immigrants. Another volunteers in a juvenile prison while a third works with pregnant teens. On Yale's campus, they are members of Campus Crusade for Christ or tutoring programs for sophomores struggling with organic chemistry. They direct plays that bring social concerns to light in a creative way and they throw an elegant to do when their best friends get engaged. In short, when my students commit to loving their neighbor and to serving those in need, I see them working towards the same goals that Christianity strives for, the kind of resolution that Harry and his world already achieved.

Questions for Your Reflection

1)   Is salvation an event or a process? Which characters are saved over time in the story and which ones receive salvation in a moment? Think of members of the Order and Dumbledore's Army, as well as Narcissa and Draco.

2)   Which salvific narrative of Jesus is most appealing? Do you think it is time and context specific? Using the characters from *Harry Potter*, do you think house-elves would respond to salvation differently than a Hogwarts student…a member of the Ministry…a wizard who had been in cahoots with Voldemort?

3)   *The Daily Prophet* tried to deny any threats to the wizarding world after Voldemort returned to bodily form at the end of *The Goblet of Fire*, thus negating a need for salvation. Did this happen at other times in the book? Do you see anything like this in our world today?

4)   Salvation, the event, happens in both the New Testament at the cross and resurrection as well as the Final Battle at Hogwarts. Why is this moment important in both stories and

what does either world look like once this salvific power has been released into the world?

5)	What does a salvific community look like? Compare the Final Battle with the beginning of the *Harry Potter* series? How has that community developed? What processes made it the vibrant force it became? Think not only of people or moments, but also of circumstances.

CHAPTER 8:

Never Trust Anything that Thinks for Itself

Revelation

Discovering Truth

I USUALLY BEGIN THE class on revelation with an exercise. Picture a grocery store checkout aisle: Three Musketeers and M&M's flank rows upon rows of magazines ranging from *People* to *The National Enquirer*. Stories about celebrity drug addictions, affairs, or secret pregnancies pepper the covers, and more often than not, we as readers peruse those shelves and think, "For real?" It becomes almost impossible to evaluate what's true and what isn't when magazine, internet, radio, and television sources all tell wildly dissimilar versions of a story. So we as information consumers are left to filter through all these sources and rely upon our own reasoning skills to figure out what to believe. Sometimes we're right on target, and sometimes we miss the mark by yards and yards. It all depends on the information we're given and how we interpret it.

If we have a hard time finding truth in stories about our celebrities and politicians, imagine how much harder it is when trying to figure out what is true about God. Since the dawn of time, humans have heard prophecies, seen visions, met angels, or listened to instructions directly from the Divine. Sometimes many members of the global community have affirmed these experiences and sometimes they have not, with the result that debate over the validity of these experiences has spawned discrimination, violence, and war.

Characters in the *Harry Potter* series also struggle to separate truth from falsehoods. Whether they trust in the Dumbledore they have experienced or the Dumbledore they've read about in Rita Skeeter's book, whether they confide in diaries or mysterious maps, every character must discern what is reliable in the wizarding world. In this chapter, we'll be looking at how Christians find truth about God and how characters in *Harry Potter* discern the truths of their world.

Defining Revelation

In the Christian vocabulary, the term "revelation" is used when discussing truths learn about God. (This is different from the Book of Revelation, which we'll discuss in the chapter on apocalypticism.) But what do Christians mean when they say that God has been revealed to them? Theologian Alister McGrath writes,

> In speaking about other persons, we might draw a distinction between "knowing about someone" and "knowing someone." The former implies cerebral knowledge, or an accumulation of data about an individual (such as her height, weight, and so on). The latter implies a personal relationship.
>
> In its developed sense, "revelation" does not mean merely the transmission of a body of knowledge, but the personal self-disclosure of God within history. God has taken the initiative through a process of self-disclosure, which reaches its climax and fulfillment in the history of Jesus of Nazareth.[33]

In this quotation, McGrath emphasizes that revelation is the process of discovering who God is in relation to

---

33   Alister E. McGrath, *Christian Theology: An Introduction, 2* (Oxford: Blackwell Publishers, 1997). 183.

humans, and that for Christians, God's identity was made clearest in Jesus. But as we will see, God can be revealed to humans in a variety of ways. We will be discussing four of these—Scripture, reason, tradition, and experience, which together are known as the Methodist Quadrilateral. Though they were codified by Charles Wesley, who founded the United Methodist denomination, they are significant for moot Chriotiano. While each of the four will be written about separately in this chapter, it is important to recognize at the outset that Christians view these as interrelated—to give just two examples, through reason Scripture is truly understood and with the help of Scripture, experience can be evaluated.

Revelation through Scripture

One of the most prominent ways that Christians come to know who God is and what God's relationship with them is happens with the help of the Bible. The Old Testament and the New Testament texts teach Christians about the promises that God made to humanity throughout history, beginning in the acts of creation and culminating in the life of Jesus of Nazareth. To be a Christian is to accept that these texts bear truth—Christians believe that the Bible recounts the mysterious and profound ways that God interacts with creation and also teaches the way that God expects humans to respond. In other words, to read this canon of books is to encounter one of the most authoritative sources of Christian belief. The Bible provides not only a history of who God has been in the past, it also offers promises about who God will continue to be in the future and gives instructions for how people should interact with one another and their creator.

If the Bible is a compilation of texts that Christians regard as authoritative, are certain texts authoritative for the wizarding world? The short answer is that there is no book of biblical proportions—pun intended—in Harry's world. The closest similarity might be *Hogwarts, A History*, which Hermione consults and memorizes with the kind of studiousness a devout Christian might have for the Bible. There is a sense that *Hogwarts, A History* provides authoritative truth about the wizarding world's identity, but even so, it is certainly not revered—except perhaps by Hermione—in the same way that most Christians revere the Bible.

Hogwarts: A History aside, many books in Harry's world seem like they ought to come with warning labels on them. Consider Snape's Potions book from *The Half-Blood Prince* as another example. Harry quickly finds that the book has a power beyond itself thanks to the tricks Snape penned in the margins. Anxious to succeed in Potions without putting in the requisite time and energy, he uses these shortcuts regularly, gaining trust in the book with each success. Though Hermione repeatedly reminds him of its dangers, Harry becomes so confident in the text that he believes it can do no harm. But that assumed trust backfires on him when he casts the *Sectumsempra* curse upon Draco Malfoy, which nearly causes him to bleed to death. Hermione jumps on Harry soon afterwards, reminding him that he ought to be more cautious when it comes to trusting unknown sources:

> "I told you there was something wrong with that Prince person," Hermione said, evidently unable to stop herself. "And I was right, wasn't I?"
>
> "No, I don't think you were," said Harry stubbornly....
>
> "Harry," said Hermione, "how can you still stick up for that book when that spell—"
>
> "Will you stop harping on about the book!" snapped Harry. "The Prince only copied it out! It's not like he was advising anyone to use it! For all we know, he was making a note of something that had been used against him!"
>
> "I don't believe this," said Hermione. "You're actually defending—"
>
> "I'm not defending what I did!" said Harry quickly. "I wish I hadn't done it, and not just because I've got about a dozen detentions. You know I wouldn't've used

a spell like that, not even with Malfoy, but you can't blame the Prince, he hadn't written 'try this out, it's really good'—he was just making notes for himself, wasn't he, not for anyone else" (*HBP*, 529-30).

If Harry's trust in Snape's *Advanced Potion-Making* book proves inappropriate, so does Ginny Weasley's trust in Tom Riddle's diary. Seeking a confidante during her first year at Hogwarts, Ginny turns to the mysterious book, which consequently possesses her and uses her to open the Chamber of Secrets. The diary becomes more powerful than anything else in her life, even the wisdom of her father, who tells her to, "Never trust anything that can think for itself *if you can't see where it keeps its brain*" (*CS*, 329). Indeed, the confidence Ginny Weasley has in the book nearly costs her life.

The final example I would like to draw upon is Rita Skeeter's biography of Dumbledore, which is published following his death. It haunts Harry, Ron, and Hermione throughout most of book seven, causing Harry especially to question basic assumptions about the wizard who had become his most trusted mentor. As a result, the book served a dangerous purpose not because it reported the ugliest parts of Dumbledore's past but because it caused Harry to doubt fundamental truths about his relationship to the wizard: was he really loved, was he really taught well? The *Life and Lies of Albus Dumbledore* held a power over Harry's worldview that was tempting in an almost demonic way, so that part of his journey in book seven was to learn to trust in the headmaster even when evidence pointed to the contrary. Without that trust, he would have lost the desire to complete the mission Dumbledore left for him.

The presence of books like these in the *Harry Potter* series implies that readers must be cautious, for books can be manipulative, especially those that possess powers beyond the words typed onto their pages. In their own way, each of these three books manipulates its reader to a negative end, by using graffiti, magical powers, or suggestive prose. It is up to the discerning reader to separate truth from falsehood using reasoning and smarts, and oftentimes, he or she fails in that task.

To summarize, it would seem that books in *Harry Potter* are not necessarily authoritative in and of themselves, given the risks that we see in these examples. Taken one step further, one might say that in Harry's world a book is only trustworthy when it empowers people to think for themselves; a non-trustworthy one takes that ability away. This means that books do not inherently reveal truth; human reasoning is needed to do that. In this way, it would seem that Harry Potter's world differs from a Christian one, given that most Christians regard the Bible as a book with truth so profound that it can provide salvation—even *Hogwarts, A History* does not make such a claim.

Revelation through Reason

Given that reasoning is an essential part of virtually every human encounter, it would be hard to imagine how one could separate truth from fiction without it. So it makes sense that many Christians believe that God can be revealed in their lives with the help of their personal reasoning skills. This opens up the possibility that what humans reason, deduce or discern about God can be truthful.

The wizarding world also holds human reasoning in high regard, but it is a tempered regard. This means that if the ability to think was so important, it would be Hermione and not Harry who saved the wizarding world, but as the books portray it, it is Harry—a character who is shown to lack exceptional intelligence—who defeats Voldemort. Hermione's brilliance was essential to Harry's mission, and yet Rowling repeatedly shows that reasoning is not an end in itself. Quite early in the series, Rowling makes the place of reasoning explicit. As Hermione tells Harry when he doubts his own intelligence, "Books! And cleverness! There are more important things—friendship and bravery" (*SS*, 287).

Yet what is essential to Hermione's intelligence is that it was in the service of the friendship and bravery she so highly prized. She used her brains for the good of her friends, staying up late to find a legal loophole that might free Buckbeak or translating *The Tales of Beedle the Bard* to help accomplish Dumbledore's mission. Other intelligent characters were not so wise: Voldemort, for instance, was reputed to be one of the most intelligent wizards of his day, yet the way in which he used his brain was destructive. Hence, reasoning only reveals truth when it is used wisely.

Christian thinkers have a similar take on this issue. They suggest that people may use their smarts in the service of Christian love or in the service of evil—i.e. a person who is good with money might create a non-profit to help people get out of debt or he might use that same noggin to engage in high-end extortion. Hence, Christians also believe that intelligence can be used for good or for ill, and that when it is used thoughtfully and carefully, it may reveal the divine.

Revelation through Tradition

Christianity has a long history during which the Church has established various traditions concerning matters such as doctrine, liturgy, and ethics. These are regarded as an authoritative source of revelation, or put differently, humans can develop a relationship with God by engaging in the traditions of the Church.

In the wizarding world, there are also traditions, some of which seem to draw the community into loving relationships with one another. The opening feast when students arrive at Hogwarts is one such example, as are the seasonal holidays and the Quidditch World Cup.

Yet the books are also skeptical of some of the ways in which wizards use tradition. Dolores Umbridge is perhaps the paradigmatic example of this: familiar with the letter of the law, she abuses it repeatedly by using the rules and institutions of the wizarding world to accomplish malicious goals. She deliberately misuses her position on the Wizengamot to punish Harry for defending himself and Dudley from the Dementors; she installs herself as the Hogwarts High Inquisitor in a blatant misuse of power in order to subjugate teachers and students who do not follow laws as she construes them. In this character, we can see how many traditions are only as salutary as those who interpret them—when traditions are used to evil ends, they become evil themselves; when they are used for good, they become that way.

Revelation through Experience

Finally, we come to experience. When Christians talk about revelatory experiences, they are referring to how God is at work in their lives. There are no rules binding these experiences, which means that they may take place at any time or in any location. Whether praying in church, singing in the shower, washing the windows, or resting on the beach, Christians believe there are no boundaries for how God is revealed to them. God may appear as a still, small voice within the heart of a faithful person, or Jesus might appear in a vision to a non-believer.

This opens up the possibility that God can be anywhere and can work in human lives in the most astonishing ways. Yet the trouble is that a lack of guidelines for judging these experiences makes it hard to evaluate their truth. Jim Jones and David Koresh serve as provocative examples. Preaching that he was the reincarnation of Jesus of Nazareth, Jim Jones amassed a following of hundreds who were so committed to his cause that they died together in the largest mass suicide in modern times; David Koresh's claim that he was a prophet drew many to his compound in Waco, Texas, eventually resulting in their death during a standoff with the United States government. How valid were the experiences of Jones and Koresh—could Jones have been the reincarnation of Jesus or Koresh a prophet because those were their experiences of God? Most Christians would take issue with the truthfulness of either claim because their practices clearly violated key tenets of Christianity—Jones's forced suicide of over 900 members of the cult and Koresh's abuse of young children certainly breach Jesus' commandment to love one's neighbor.

But while these are extreme examples of the ways in which personal experiences of the divine can be exploited, other cases prove more ambiguous. People may feel called by God to take a certain political stance while others may feel God is asking them to take the opposite stance. One individual may sense that God is constantly present during hardships while another has a sense of God's absence during the same trial. These situations prove that one person's experience of God can be vastly different from another's, and this makes it seem as if God works contradictory ways.

This makes experience the most tenuous of all the forms of revelation. Unlike Scripture (which is a concrete body of knowledge), or reason (which operates by socially agreed-upon rules), or tradition (which can be traced through its two-thousand-year development), experience is rooted entirely within the individual, bound by neither text nor history. Because it is so personal, it can be the most compelling of the sources, but since it fluctuates from person to person, it can also be the most unreliable.

Harry and Draco's relationship to Dumbledore and the ideals of love and tolerance models this. Whereas Harry experienced Dumbledore as someone who taught and showed him love, Draco experienced him as antagonistic. Likewise, Harry's experience of Dumbledore was antithetical to the Dumbledore portrayed in Rita Skeeter's book, and the dissonance that Harry experiences because of this leads to his own crisis of faith: his own life was evidence that Dumbledore fought for the values of love and tolerance, but the book said otherwise.

This is perhaps why experience needs the other sources to evaluate its validity both in Christianity and in Harry's world. Just as Christians interpret their experiences in light of how they relate to Scripture, reason, or tradition, so do characters in the books. Hermione, for example, considers the validity of Rita Skeeter's book in light of her experience and intellectual knowledge of Dumbledore. This process ultimately allows her to maintain trust in Dumbledore and the mission he left them.

Experience and Belief

Belief can often begin with a profound experience of God, what some Christians call being "born again" or a "coming to Jesus" moment. Yet many others believe without such an encounter.

Like Christians, some characters in Harry's world believe in the ideals of love *because* of their experiences whereas others believe even in the absence of evidence. Neville Longbottom exemplifies this in an elegant way: he believes in the ideals of love that Dumbledore and Harry stand for throughout the entire series, but most stridently when those values seem near obliteration—in the darkest days of the war. Neville never loses faith; his belief in those ideals doesn't even waver after Harry's death, since Rowling writes that after Voldemort announces Harry's demise to those at Hogwarts, Neville breaks away from the crowd and rushes towards Voldemort. The villain tempts Neville by offering him a place as a Death Eater, but Neville holds fast to what he knows to be true: "I'll join you when hell freezes over," he responds (*DH*, 731). Voldemort then tries to sway Neville to the other side, as if to say that because love and tolerance cannot win, he should betray the cause. Yet Neville demonstrates that he will continue to believe in those values even when Harry's death is overwhelming evidence that their cause is lost. His faith never fails him..

Luna Lovegood is another character who believes despite a lack of evidence. Like Neville, she is faithful to the values Harry stands for, so faithful that she and Neville alone continue to check the DA coins when others have long ago forgotten them. Luna also has faith in another central truth in the series: that death cannot trump love. Rowling portrays this most poignantly at the end of book five, as Harry grieves the loss of his godfather. He meets Luna searching for the belongings her schoolmates hid, when Harry asks her about her dead mother. In the following interchange, Luna shows the depth of her faith in more ways than one:

> "I still feel very sad about it sometimes. But I've still got Dad. And anyway, it's not as though I'll never see Mum again, is it?"

> "Er—isn't it?" said Harry uncertainly.

> She shook her head in disbelief. "Oh, come on. You heard them just behind the veil, didn't you?"

> "You mean…"

> "In that room with the archway. They were just lurking out of sight, that's all. You heard them."

They looked at each other. Luna was smiling slightly. Harry did not know what to say, or to think. Luna believed so many extraordinary things…yet he had been sure he had heard voices behind the veil too….

"Are you sure you don't want me to help you look for your stuff?" he said.

"Oh no," said Luna. "No, I think I'll just go down and have some pudding and wait for it all to turn up…. It always does in the end….Well, have a nice holiday, Harry" (*OP*, 864).

Luna demonstrates her faith in two things during that interchange, one simple and one profound. First, she believes that her belongings will reappear and because of that, she doesn't need to go searching for them; she has faith that they will be there when she needs them, despite the evidence that they have disappeared. This becomes a metaphor for how she understands death: just because she cannot see the dead does not mean that they are not present, and just because the laws of magic say that no one can return from death does not mean that the living and those behind the veil cannot interact. Luna does not need evidence to believe, and as shown by her dire commitment to Crumple-Horned Snorkacks and Umgubular Slashkilters, she is capable of believing in even the most unlikely causes.

Interestingly, both Luna and Neville also demonstrate the kind of faith C.S. Lewis writes about in his essay, "On Obstinacy in Belief." In this essay, Lewis makes a distinction between the role evidence plays in coming to belief in the first place, and the role it plays in maintaining belief thereafter. He suggests that people believe they have good evidence when they come to a belief, whether it be based in Scripture, reason, tradition, or experience. (In Lewis's case, he began to believe in God on the basis of logical arguments—arguments rooted in reason—that he felt were irrefutable.) Yet once a person adopts faith, evidence is no longer needed to maintain it, which means that it comes to play a different role. To illustrate what Lewis meant, Professor John Hare of Yale University gave this analogy: imagine your friend—who has always been reliable and trustworthy in the past—promised to meet you for dinner, but he's late. Do you wait for him or not? Given that you trust him, you recognize that something important delayed him and he will likely arrive shortly. In other words, because your friend has given you evidence in the past that he is reliable, your belief in him does not waver when he is late, even though you have no evidence in that moment to support that he is a good friend. This is the way that Luna and Neville operate; even when evidence disappears, they trust in the ideals of love, and so they trust Harry Potter.[34]

But there's a catch to the friend analogy and to Lewis's argument: imagine your friend doesn't show up. Two days go by, and you're waiting for him, hoping that he will arrive because you believe in him. In the meantime, the food has gotten cold and is starting to rot; you are starving. Your friend has not called and when you call around, you hear that it is not because an emergency came up. When you finally hear from your friend, you invite him over a second time, and again he doesn't appear. At a point like this, it is no longer rational to trust your friend, and it might make more sense to become suspicious, wondering what has gotten into him or why he doesn't like you. You might not want to be his friend anymore because you don't want to put up with people who are so disrespectful of your time. So as evidence accumulates that your friend is not the trustworthy person you thought he was, you might begin to re-evaluate your beliefs about him. In Christianity, people often feel this way during experiences of evil: who God was at other times in their lives does not seem the same as who God is during their difficulties, and this leads to a crisis of faith.

This is also how Harry feels during book seven. Prior evidence suggests that Dumbledore stands for love and inclusion, that he can answer most questions and solve most problems, that he has Harry's back. But his sudden death followed by Rita Skeeter's publication puts all of this into question for Harry. Dumbledore becomes like the late dinner guest and Harry like the friend who must now decide whether to continue trusting. What Harry's journey through book seven teaches the reader

---

34   John Hare. Lecture. Yale University. October 11, 2006.

is the importance of trusting or believing even when evidence points to the contrary. For some characters, like Neville and Luna, this is a flawless journey, whereas for others like Harry, it is a challenging one.

Pascal and his Wager

One last note about belief from a name that may be familiar to you: Blaise Pascal of Pascal's famous wager. Pascal's wager states that one should choose the thing that has the most gain and the least risk. So, for instance, if you believe in God, you could gain eternal life and the risk is that some humans will disapprove of your choice. If you don't believe in God, you might have more fun on earth because you wouldn't have to adhere to God's ethical guidelines, but you would risk an eternity in hell...and some people still wouldn't like you! Pascal therefore says that it's in a person's best interest to believe in God because therein lies the greatest gain—the possibility of eternal life.

Pascal's line of reasoning has its problems: for instance, what if one puts faith in the wrong things thinking they're the right things. Take Bellatrix Lestrange. No one was more committed to Voldemort's cause than Bellatrix, and yet because she made the wrong choice—because she sided with prejudice over love—the outcome wasn't as she expected. Bellatrix's case shows that human judgment can be frail and faulty, so that even when we think we've reasoned through a situation, we can still make serious errors.

But perhaps the greatest problem with Blaise Pascal's line of reasoning is that it seems to overlook the role of sincerity. A person who chooses God because that option offers the greatest personal gain may not actually believe in the tenets of faith. Is that person a believer in the same way as another person who is committed to those ideals? This model assumes that she is, but that may not be the correct assumption to make.

The *Harry Potter* books also seem wary of hedging a bet like this, as illustrated by the depiction of Horace Slughorn. As a classic example of Pascal's wager, Slughorn makes decisions because of their convenience and not their truth. He returns to Hogwarts because Dumbledore persuades him with guarantees of glamour and safety, not because he is truly committed to teaching Potions or defending students from the Dark Lord. Likewise, though he aligns himself with Dumbledore in theory, his actions protect memories of Voldemort that provide information necessary for his defeat, so that only with the help of Felix Felicis are those memories extracted.

Though by the end of book seven he rallies members of Slytherin house to fight against Voldemort and even takes arms against his former student, one will always wonder whether Slughorn sided with Dumbledore's Army because he agreed with their ideals or because it was in his best interest to do so. The reader will never know. But it is telling that few readers hold Horace Slughorn in the same regard as Neville and Luna. There is a qualitative difference between the beliefs of these characters, and the reader senses it. One is motivated by selfishness and the other by sincerity, and as in Christianity, it is sincerity that wins the day.

The Truth Is...

Like many other people, students in my class struggle with what to believe about God. Some of them come from households infused with faith and others from homes where even talk of religion is shunned. Some of them find faith easy to come by, and others find it nearly impossible.

One such student comes to mind for whom this was the case. I met with her on an overcast afternoon at Claire's, a local restaurant with incredible desserts. Over two slices of cake—one Lithuanian coffee and the other chocolate banana—we talked about her final paper. But the topic shifted as our time together passed, moving from revelation in *Harry Potter* to revelation in her life. "I wish I could believe in something," she said, "But every time I try, it's like an empty void. I never feel God's presence; I never sense there's anything there." And then, as if she was nervous that someone would judge her, she quickly continued, "But I want to. It seems so easy for other people. I don't know why it's so hard for me."

I could tell that my student was frustrated—she'd read

the Bible and other religious texts; she'd experimented with everything from the Jewish Sabbath to the Christian Christmas to Zen meditation, looking for a sparkle of the divine. But nothing worked for her. What I told my student was that she wasn't alone in her experiences, that belief is hard for many people, even those whose faith might seem sure. Then, at the risk of taking Harry and his friends a bit too seriously, I asked, "What helps the *Harry Potter* characters find faith?"

She paused for a few moments, started and stopped sentences as she worked out this question in her head. Then she smiled. "Their friends," she said. "The people around them. When they hang out or play Quidditch or solve mysteries together, they get a glimpse of love from one another."

So I told my student that if attending religious services, praying to an abstract entity, or reading from a holy book were too overwhelming for her, perhaps she should start with something more concrete—her experiences in the world—and then maybe belief would come to her when she wasn't looking for it.

This is exactly what happens in the *Harry Potter* books. It's not that Ron, Harry, Hermione, or others are divine; it's that they're open to letting love work in and through them. They let themselves feel love and give it to others, so that it can be passed on like a contagious disease. By doing this repeatedly, they come to believe that love is, well, worth believing in.

What the books seem to be saying is to look for love in this world, inside those things that are intimate to you, and there you shall find it. Because of this, the actions and attitudes of characters in the series matter. Draco Malfoy does not discover love's power because he is inherently incapable but because he refuses to be open to the possibility—rejecting Dumbledore's offer of love and protection on the top of the astronomy tower is perhaps the most poignant example of this. Likewise, Harry allows himself to feel the power of love, even though he knows loving can be painful, as he discovers with the death of Sirius and others.

How is it that some characters seem to be able to trust in the power of love while others seem incapable? This is one of the most disturbing questions Christians struggle with, as well as one of the most challenging ones we can pose to the *Harry Potter* books.

Our next chapter on grace will hopefully provide some clues.

Questions for Your Reflection

1) What ways do "divine" messages seem to come to *Harry Potter* characters? How was their "divinity" determined?

2) Is the prophecy found in Divinations a type of revelation? The prophecy concerning Dumbledore and Harry? Concerning this situation, was there stronger revelation involved?

3) Given there is not the equivalent of Scripture in *Harry Potter*, how do you think different characters would have interpreted a sacred text like the Bible?

4) Does circumstance make faith in a certain revelation easier? Think of these questions in terms of family backgrounds, the races present in *Harry Potter*, the amount of danger involved in one's life, and your own story.

5) In what other ways did *Harry Potter* characters open or close themselves off to the power of Love? Reflect on changes that occurred over the series.

CHAPTER 9:

Lighting the Deluminator

Grace

Grace and Grades

As this story will show, there's a bit of Hermione in me. I took my first theology class during sophomore year. I worked hard in it, but I didn't know much about this new discipline, and most of the people in the class had a stronger background than I did. I wanted to do well, but I didn't know how, and I worried that if I didn't get a good grade then I'd feel that I was letting myself down. Or worse yet, everyone else, whoever the 'everyone else' who saw my transcript actually were.

So I took notes in that class like they were directions for fighting off a deadly disease, and I spent so many hours studying for its papers and exams that I had a recurring dream of skydiving with Martin Luther and Aquinas. Definitely a sign that I was taking things too seriously! But despite the effort, I was never able to break that barrier between just getting by and really knowing my stuff. So, frustrated when I got a lower-than-average-for-me grade on a paper, I went to speak to the professor, not because I wanted a change in the mark, but because I needed an explanation, some way to do better, some way to fix what I'd been doing wrong.

"I don't understand," I said. "I did all the reading, and I spent hours on this paper, and I tried to explain what was at

stake in Aquinas's theology of Mary's virgin conception, and…
.I….I…I'm so confused."

And at that moment, to my utter mortification, I broke into tears. And not just a couple of tears either. This was full out, uncontrollable sobbing, the kind that makes your sinuses throb and your cheeks burn.

That to me was almost worse than the grade. I didn't want to admit that I had weaknesses regardless of whether they were intellectual or emotional, and I certainly didn't want my professor to think that I was trying to sob my way to an A. All I'd wanted was to have a rational conversation about how to fix whatever mysterious mistakes I was making, but instead, I found myself with my head in my hands, crying the way exhausted and overworked people do: with reckless abandon.

My professor rose from her desk and crossed to the other side to sit next to me. Then she put one hand on my head and said, "Danielle, God doesn't care about what grade you get in this class, and neither should you. The grades will come. Concentrate on flourishing. That's what makes you shine."

I left her office red-eyed, wiped out, and feeling worse than I had before. But her words stayed with me. They were the last thing I contemplated before going to sleep that night, and when I finally closed my eyes, it was to a deeper slumber, not to dreams about airborne adventures with deceased theologians! In the coming years, I tried to take those words to heart until they became so much a part of who I was that my whole attitude towards learning changed. It became about being passionate for something, not impressing anyone. My professor gave me the freedom to make that change.

This story is a simple one about two people, but it's also a great analogy for how Christians understand grace. Historically, grace is defined as a free gift from God that changes person's disposition so that it's dominated by love instead of sin. It differs from mercy, which is God's unmerited forgiveness for a wrongdoing. Grace isn't God acting to absolve inappropriate action; it is God giving a gift that changes the heart. So God replaces sinful dispositions with wholesome ones, just as my professor showed me graciousness and helped shape my outlook on grades and self-worth.

We're going to begin this chapter with some different Christian understandings of how humans receive this gift. Then we're going to apply these different ideas about grace to the *Harry Potter* books to see which are privileged. Ready? Because there's going to be a test at the end, and if you don't get an A, then you can't go onto the next chapter.

Kidding.

Grace in the Augustinian Tradition

Most Christians believe that the work of salvation begins at Jesus' crucifixion but culminates at the resurrection. This ascent from the dead is the definitive sign that Jesus has defeated sin and conquered evil; these forces can no longer have the same power over humans once Jesus has shown that they can be transformed into new life. When people receive this fruit of Jesus' work, they say that they have been graced.

In the Augustinian view of sin, God bestows grace upon people who are incapable of acquiring it for themselves. This makes sense if we recall how Augustine thought that humans are born into a state of sin. It's a given, non-negotiable. Likewise, they can be held responsible for the evils they commit. Given this construction of human nature, it makes sense that humans cannot procure grace on their own, and it shows how consistent Augustine is about what he keeps in his suitcase and what he disregards.

But if everyone is in the same boat when it comes to being tainted by sin and if God bestows grace upon humans, then how come everyone doesn't seem to experience grace? From experience, we know that some people have a sense of that gift in their lives, but many others do not. When we consider Augustine's view of grace from the perspective of human experience, we see that the biggest item he leaves out of the suitcase is an explanation for why God seems so arbitrary in the allocation of grace, why some people feel as if they experience God's gift while others do not. This is something that Pelagius and C.S. Lewis both address in their conceptions of grace.

Grace and Pelagius

We've already discussed one big controversy in the early Christian tradition: the Arian heresy. Now let's turn to a slightly later one. The Pelagian controversy.

The Pelagian controversy erupted in the fifth century when the theologian Pelagius suggested that humans were capable of becoming sinless by perfecting themselves. According to Pelagius, individuals were born without sin and had the capability to permanently avoid it. This contradicts Augustine's understanding of original sin, that which tainted all humans from birth.

One of the consequences of Pelagius's thought had to do with the way that God interacted with people. Pelagius suggested that God provided information to humans about how to live morally, using tools like the Ten Commandments or the life of Jesus. However, God took a pretty hands-off approach when it came to individual lives. After imparting the necessary information, God let humans do their own thing and would only intervene again in the end times, at the final judgment.

What works about Pelagius's approach is that it appeals to our experience of our own free will. We seem to be autonomous creatures, capable of making our own decisions, many of which are good. That said, experience also shows that some people seem utterly incapable of making morally conscientious decisions while others may be resolute in making them but unable to follow through. It just doesn't seem possible for a person to make responsible decisions *all* the time. Even when we know what's best for us—not to eat that cookie, not to drive above the speed limit—sometimes we just can't help ourselves. In other words, nobody's perfect, though Pelagius seems to think we could be.

Additionally, Augustine critiqued Pelagius by saying that he was ignoring a majority of the New Testament, especially when it came to what that canon had to say about Jesus. For instance, John 15:5 says, "Apart from me you can do nothing." Quotations like this directly contradict the way Pelagius understood human abilities. Moreover, the New Testament also says that Jesus died and was resurrected to provide grace and salvation. As texts like John 3:17 say, "God did not send the

Son into the world to condemn the world, but in order that the world might be saved through him." So if people could achieve all that themselves, then why was Jesus' sacrifice so essential?

For all these reasons, Pelagius's ideas about grace, sin and the human condition quickly fell out of favor in theological circles while Augustine's theologies became increasingly prominent. Though Augustine's view of grace remains one of the most widely accepted, there is one final, more recent thinker that I would like us to think about before we consider how grace operates in *Harry Potter*.

C.S. Lewis

Like others before him, C.S. Lewis frequently used fiction as a means to convey his theological ideas. Though his most famous book may be *The Lion, the Witch, and the Wardrobe*, Lewis composed a number of works that deal with prominent issues in Christian thought, and of these, *The Great Divorce* is one. The novel begins with a dream Lewis has of boarding a bus that takes him and others from the grey town they are in to a giant field. The people, who are dead and translucent, have different reactions to the field. Some of them run immediately back to the bus; some explore but decide they don't like it; some interact with solid people—reps from Heaven—who try to persuade them to walk through the field to Paradise, but the task seems too daunting and they retreat. Of those who boarded the bus, only one takes the plunge, a man with a lizard on his shoulder. This man is approached by one of the solid people, an angel, who asks why the man plans to return to the grey town. When the man says it is because of the lizard on his shoulder, the angel offers to kill the beast, but the man refuses. Over the course of several pages, the man offers excuses for why the angel can't kill his companion: it would hurt or he would die too, being the most prominent. Despite the fact that the angel tells him again and again that nothing will happen to him but that the lizard must die if he is to permanently leave grey town, the man is reluctant. Finally, this interchange occurs:

'Have I permission?' said the Angel to the Ghost.

'I know it will kill me.'

'It won't. But supposing it did?'

'You're right. It would be better to be dead than to live with this creature.'

'Then I may?'

'Damn and blast you! Go on, can't you? Get it over. Do what you like,' bellows the Ghost: but ended, whimpering, 'God help me. God help me.'

Next moment the Ghost gave a scream of agony such as I never heard on Earth. The Burning One closed his crimson grip on the reptile: twisted it, while it bit and writhed, and then flung it, broken-backed, on the turf.[35]

The lizard is ripped from the man following his acquiescence, and immediately thereafter, the man loses his ghost-like appearance and becomes solid while the lizard turns into a horse. The man then mounts the horse and together he and the angel depart for Heaven.

In this story, the lizard is a metaphor for the man's sins, and only once he agrees to shed that crutch is he able to receive God's grace and heavenly reward. In other words, what Lewis is saying is that grace may be God's gift, but it is a gift that humans must be willing to accept. Only once they say, "Yes, this is for me," can God step in and bestow the offering.

This kind of theology of grace might be said to be a middle ground between Augustine and Pelagius. Like Pelagius, Lewis proposes that humans do have a role in obtaining God's gift, only it is not as substantive as that early theologian believed: instead of procuring grace for themselves, humans must take the small step of asking for it. Only once they have made the request can the gift be received. Likewise,

---

35   C.S. Lewis, *The Great Divorce* (New York: HarperCollins, 1973). 110.

Lewis privileges Augustinian thought by acknowledging that humans don't do all the work themselves, and indeed they are incapable of doing it all themselves. His theology, therefore, maintains a blend between the best ideas of each thinker.

Grace in Harry's world

The big question we're going to ask here is whether Augustine, Pelagius, or C.S. Lewis's understanding of grace is present in the series. If Augustine or C.S. Lewis, we can make the argument that the book's ideas about grace match Christianity's. But if it's the third of these authors, then we might see that the books portray human abilities in a way that Christianity opposes.

Let's begin with Augustine. Are there characters in the series who receive a free gift that allows them to transcend their prejudices and isolation, which, as we said earlier, is the heart of sin in the wizarding world? Draco Malfoy seems the most likely candidate. Rescued from the burning pyre in the Room of Requirement during the Battle at Hogwarts, Draco is spared the fate he deserves, and is instead given the opportunity to live a free and unfettered life in the wizarding world following the Dark Lord's demise. He does nothing to ask for that gift, and he certainly does not deserve it. So is this an example of Augustinian grace at work?

Potentially yes, potentially no. The trouble is that we don't know what happens to Malfoy's disposition in his adult years. Rowling leaves his description ambiguous, making us wonder whether he has changed his priorities or whether he merely cloaks them, recognizing that they are no longer appropriate to voice. If the latter, then no, he has not received grace because his sinful constitution—which still believes in exclusion and isolation—has not been transformed. We could say that he received mercy because he was spared the fate he deserved, but this is different from grace. Grace involves a gift from God that changes the deepest parts of the human heart. Mercy is being spared a punishment.

As for Pelagianism, we will not do much better there. No one in the series becomes inclusive and communal purely on their own—characters like Harry, Dumbledore, Ron and Neville are able to grow into that disposition because of the active guidance of love. Take Ron Weasley. When Ron abandons Hermione and Harry, he may have wanted to return immediately, but he needed the help of the Deluminator. As Ron tells Harry and Hermione:

> "So I took it out," Ron went on, looking at the Deluminator, "and it didn't seem different or anything, but I was sure I'd heard you [through it]. So I clicked it. And the light went out in my room, but another light appeared right outside the window."
>
> Ron raised his empty hand and pointed in front of him, his eyes focused on something neither Harry nor Hermione could see.
>
> "It was a ball of light, kind of pulsing, and bluish, like that light you get around a Portkey, you know?"
>
> "Yeah," said Harry and Hermione together automatically.
>
> "I knew this was it," said Ron. "I grabbed my stuff and packed it, then I put on my rucksack and went out into the garden...."
>
> "It sort of floated toward me," said Ron, illustrating the movement with his free index finger, "right to my chest, and then—it just went straight through. It was here," he touched a point close to his heart, "I could feel it, it was hot. And once it was inside me I knew what I was supposed to do, I knew it would take me where I needed to go. So I Disapparated and came out on the side of a hill" (*DH*, 384-5).

Here we see that the Deluminator didn't create a change in Ron—he had to make the effort to pack his bags and walk through the light. But we also see that Ron didn't do all the work to overcome his insecurities and have a change of heart. The Deluminator had to be there in order for Ron to shed his metaphoric lizard and say, "Yes, this is fo me." In other words, Ron's experience of receiving grace and accepting a new way of being was more in line with C.S. Lewis's construct of grace than with either Augustine's or Pelagius's.

Indeed, most of the grace-like moments in the books are depicted in a way that resonates with Lewis. Dumbledore transforms from someone who values superiority to someone who believes in inclusiveness because his sister's death gave him an opportunity to change his worldview and he took it; Kreacher becomes accepting of Harry, Hermione, Ron and their mission when Harry gives him Sirius' necklace and he agrees to take it; Harry is able to defeat Voldemort because again and again he chooses to follow the path love sets for him. In contrast, characters like Bellatrix and the Carrows never experience grace because they have no desire to, and likewise Voldemort never receives it because, even in his dying moments, he will not repent. That Voldemort is even given the choice to change after all the atrocities he committed shows that grace in the wizarding world can be extended to even the great sinner—as it can in Christianity—but it also shows that grace must be welcomed to take effect. In other words, characters who evidence some sort of inner transformation make that transformation because of a combination of two things: a free gift offered and a choice to receive it. Those without it refused to accept the gift.

Choosing Grace

What we can conclude from this is that the series does not privilege either Augustine's historically dominant view of grace or Pelagius's heretical one. Rather, the books formulate grace from a more modern perspective that matches Lewis's idea that grace is a free gift that must be chosen. In this manner, we also see another way in which the series highlights the importance of choice and free will.

I've made a choice myself, now that I'm in my professor's shoes: I try to interact with my students the way she did with me. When they share their fears about papers, I reiterate the heart of my professor's message—find what you love about a paper and use that as your motivation to write. It will result in a better paper than anything you'd assemble with a different mindset. And remember: it's just a grade. As Hogwart's resident brainiac reminds us, "There are more important things" (*SS*, 287).

Questions for Your Reflection

1)   What is the difference between grace and graciousness? Is it more common for Rowling to write about graciousness among the characters than an event of grace for any one character? What are some of these moments?

2)   What is the role of grace in relation to sacrifice? Think of Lily's sacrifice for Harry and how Harry came to relate to that sacrifice.

3)   Using C.S. Lewis' "lizard" metaphor, what form do you think that animal takes for some *Harry Potter* characters? Have some characters undergone a process of transformation like the lizard man does? Think about Gilderoy Lockhart, Bellatrix Lestrange, and Horace Slughorn. Now, think of Albus Dumbledore, Remus Lupin, Minerva McGonagall, and Cedric Diggory.

4)   Which character most supports Pelagius' thoughts on grace? Does he or she support Pelagius completely?

5)   How does C.S. Lewis' theology of grace relate to the Happy Exchange model of salvation from chapter 6? Does any *Harry Potter* character exemplify this?

CHAPTER 10:

Something Wicked This Way Comes

The End Times

The Beginning of the End

THE END TIMES IS one of the most provocative topics in modern Christian thought and also one of the most enthusiastic in the classroom. As we will see, there are many parallels between the images used in the series and those in the Book of Revelation, but to fully appreciate their significance, we need to establish some background information, beginning with the difference between two key terms in our discussion: apocalypse and eschatology. Oftentimes these words are used interchangeably, but they are in fact different things. Eschatology is a term used by theologians to refer to anything relating to the end times; the word apocalypse comes from the Greek meaning "something revealed," so it makes sense that this literature is specifically interested in what will happen after the eschaton—which means the end of time—is revealed. Scholars consider apocalyptic literature to be a subset of eschatological thought that is characterized by certain themes we will discuss below. Broadly speaking, all apocalyptic literature is considered eschatological. In contrast, not all eschatological literature is considered apocalyptic.

Because the Book of Revelation is the most widely discussed piece of Christian apocalyptic writing, we will take a look at some of the images that appear in Revelation and see how they are also used in the *Harry Potter* books. But before we get to that, let's take a brief tour through the history of apocalyptic thought. Since I'll be suggesting that the *Harry Potter* series are an example of this kind of writing, we'll also look at some of its characteristics to see how they appear in Rowling's writing.

History of Christian Apocalyptic Literature

Apocalyptic literature is first and foremost considered to be the literature of an oppressed people, so it makes sense that these writings began in the Judeo-Christian traditions around the time of one of the earliest crises of the Jewish people: the Babylonian conquest of Jerusalem in 586 BCE. The Babylonian invasion resulted in the destruction of the Jewish temple in Jerusalem as well as the exile of a number of Jewish people from their homeland. Jewish thinkers at the time viewed the loss as catastrophic because it signaled that their god was not as powerful as the Babylonian god Marduk, so during the time of the exile, a number of texts were written that were indignant about the Temple's destruction. These texts insisted that the Jewish people would be vindicated, and that their oppression would not last. When Cyrus the Great of Persia finally defeated the Babylonians in 538 BCE, the Jewish people took it as a sign that Yahweh had triumphed over Marduk after all.

Many of the writings from the Exile were canonized in the Old Testament, and in them we see the emerging essence of apocalyptic thought: that God will liberate the oppressed and the opposing party will be punished. As history progressed and the Jewish people experienced other instances of subjugation, this sentiment became more developed; it is at its most prominent in the Book of Daniel, which deals with the Babylonian Exile and also foretells the later Destruction of the Altar in the Second Temple.

The idea that the innocent will be liberated and the oppressor revenged is without doubt the most emblematic characteristic of apocalyptic literature, but there are some other important themes worth highlighting as well. The first, as we touched upon in the introduction, is that apocalyptic literature always has to do with the end times, and in particular, it often seeks to resolve what happens after death. Second, apocalyptic literature stresses that God's love and power endures, even in times of suffering. This provides assurance that the good—supported by God—will triumph over evil, and that the evil will receive vengeance. This characteristic is intimately related to the third—pessimistic optimism. This ironic phrase signifies that things must get worse before they get better; hence, you may be optimistic that your leg will heal when it is broken, but you also know that you're going to be in a lot of pain first because you need four surgeries before you can walk again. In the context of apocalyptic literature, this means that oppressed people are certain that God will ultimately triumph over the captor, but before that happens, the situation will likely worsen.

Finally, apocalyptic literature usually issues a call for loyalty. In times of difficulty, the repressed party must bond together rather than fragment, and they must form a community rather than dissolve under stress or provocation from the captor. Most importantly, they must not lose faith in God, who will ultimately triumph and vindicate them.

Within the Christian New Testament, these themes are most prominently displayed in the Book of Revelation. This apocalyptic narrative draws heavily from the Jewish tradition, and it emphasizes the importance of judgment and salvation: those who erred will be judged and those who are innocent will be saved. The key difference between this text and its Jewish predecessors is the presence of Jesus as Messiah.[36]

The Book of Revelation—please note that it is not Revelations—is the concluding book in the New Testament and said to be written by John of Patmos to the churches in the western part of modern-day Turkey. The book is intended to give these early persecuted Christians hope for the future, and to do that John paints a picture in which Old Testament prophecies are fulfilled: redemption will occur for believers,

---

36   For more detailed information on apocalyptic literature, see John Collin's *Apocalyptic Imagination: An Introduction to Jewish Apocalyptic Literature.* Grand Rapids, MI: Wm. B. Eerdmans Publishing Company. 1998.

martyrs will be rewarded, and good will triumph. There are many vibrant images within Revelation that have become hallmarks of Christian apocalyptic thought. As we segue into our discussion of the *Harry Potter* series, we will draw upon some of these images to show their relevance to the books.

The Symbolism of Revelation

There are a number of striking images in the Book of Revelation that have become hallmarks of Christian apocalyptic thought. As we look through some of these images and their relationship to Rowling's world, please keep in mind that because these symbols have become so ingrained in the Christian worldview, they have also seeped into secular discourse in a variety of ways. For instance, while the snake represents evil in Revelation and other parts of the Bible, it has a similar characterization in the secular world. It will therefore be hard to prove that these symbols are associated with Revelation because of how they share meanings in both the secular and religious spheres. Nonetheless, it is worth remarking upon the similarities between *Harry Potter* and Revelation because the invocation of so many apocalyptic images does seem to reinforce a specifically Christian reading of the end times.

Themes from Revelation

The Harry Potter series is a story about oppression: We know that Christian apocalyptic literature is interested in how God will vindicate the captive and punish the captor. The *Harry Potter* series asks the same question. This saga takes the reader through Harry's childhood in order to prove that those who stand for the ideals of equality, tolerance, and love—in other words, the good guys—may be oppressed by Voldemort's powers, but they will not be conquered. Mudbloods and members of Dumbledore's Army are threatened, tortured, suppressed, and even killed. The Ministry of Magic becomes infiltrated with corruption, and St. Mungo's must have been full to capacity with the Imperiused. These examples show that at its heart the series, like the Book of Revelation, is looking at the fate of an oppressed people, and as in *Harry Potter* the vindication of the righteous and love's defeat over death are explicitly attested to in the biblical book. Hence, John writes, "Then I saw a new heaven and a new earth; for the first heaven and the first earth had passed away…Death will be no more; mourning and crying and pain will be no more, for the first things have passed away" (Rev. 21:1, 4). If Revelation paints an unimaginably optimistic picture of the end times, so does *Harry Potter*: in the epilogue to book seven, the reader cannot help but feel that Harry and his friends have lived their adult years in the kind of "new earth" that John writes about.

The Harry Potter series is a story about the end times: In Christianity, the end times are marked by a changing world order that inaugurates God's kingdom of peace. This is particularly pronounced in the Book of Revelation, which says that at the end times, the faithful will be persecuted, and through a war, they will defeat those who work against God's will. We see the same kind of framework in Harry's world: Voldemort's rise to power results in a war with those who are faithful to the ideals of love and tolerance. At the end of those battles, a reign of peace begins that seems to mark a new world order. When read in this way, the epilogue in book seven, which some consider sappy and overly optimistic, is given new meaning: it signifies that Harry is living in peace, without the conflict and violence that pervaded his youth. (Some of my students also found this ending saccharine or annoying, but when read with Revelation in mind, they appreciated why an ending like this is fitting, even if they would have written it differently!) Along with the alleviation of physical violence, Harry also seems psychologically and emotionally healed. The reader notices this most in Harry's attitude toward the houses at Hogwarts and in the name of his son. Whereas Harry once pledged exclusive allegiance to Gryffindor House and held fast to an unmitigated hatred of Slytherin, he now holds a more nuanced view of the houses, recognizing that each holds the possibility for a deep and abiding morality, but that they are only as good as the choices their members make. The name of his son, Albus Severus, is also symbolic of Harry's fulfillment because it signifies that he has overcome the distrust he once had towards his two most dedicated advocates—Snape and Dumbledore. Characters other than Harry also seem to resolve the conflicts that kept them from wholeness—Hermione marries Ron, Neville becomes a professor, and Teddy Lupin lives a healthy, vibrant life despite the death of his parents. Likewise, there is punishment: Draco Malfoy may still be alive, but as Harry watches him from Platform 9 ¾, there is a sense that he lacks the community and inner peace that others found. These examples from the epilogue all show the way in which the end of book seven accomplishes the same end as the Book of Revelation: it tells a story about a cosmic conflict at the end of an age that ultimately inaugurates a reign of peace. Of course, if the reader finds the epilogue sugary, it's understandable because sadly, peace never makes for a good story!

Love's power endures all in the Harry Potter series: There are no certainties from the perspective of the characters in Harry's world; however, the reader, especially the discerning reader who peruses the books more than once, can see that the series had a grand plan, an inevitable conclusion that everything from book one led up to. This is not just the hallmark of excellent writing. It shows that even in Harry's darkest hours, there were lessons to be learned about the enduring power of a love that can even conquer death. The reader recognizes that Harry's seven-year long journey has been to teach him the purpose of loving well, and only once he has truly mastered what it means to love his neighbor and himself, can he make a sacrifice that transforms other members of the wizarding world. Was Harry's sacrifice determined? There's no evidence that it was any more determined than any of our actions are. But what is clear is that at the apex of this story, we see that love was always with Harry and his friends, even in their greatest struggles, and that love's power could never be vanquished.

Characters in the Harry Potter series issue a call for loyalty: Characters throughout the series possess a strong sense of loyalty, especially when it comes to protecting one another from Voldemort. Organizations like Dumbledore's Army and the Order of the Pheonix exist so that enemies of Voldemort can band together and fight for shared values. Within Hogwarts, the strong friendships between students provide a basis for lifelong loyalty to one another. Voldemort, too, requires commitment from his followers, so that characters in the series must make a conscious choice between two loyalties: are they with Voldemort or Harry, with the ideals of prejudice or love?

Pessimistic optimism in the Harry Potter series: Of the eschatological themes, this is the one least evident in the books. While Revelation and other apocalyptic biblical books imply that the faithful have a sense of optimism during their trials, Harry and others in the series experience deep doubt about their future. Book seven contains little evidence that Harry or his friends feel certain of a positive outcome in the battle against Voldemort. Of course, one must bear in mind the literary element here: the books would be far less tense and gripping if characters were assured victory.

Symbols from Revelation

In addition to themes from Revelation, the *Harry Potter* series also alludes to certain images from this text:

The Mark of the Beast: One of the most famous images in Revelation is the Mark of the Beast, which appears in chapter 13 of the biblical text. It says that the Mark, "Causes all, both small and great, both rich and poor, both free and slave, to be marked on the right hand or the forehead, so that no one can buy or sell who does not have the mark, that is, the name of the beast or the number of its name" (Rev. 13:16-7). What is interesting for our purposes is that the Mark of the Beast bears a striking resemblance to the Dark Mark imprinted on Voldemort's followers and illuminating the sky above the places Voldemort kills. It may also be alluded to in the scar on Harry's forehead. All of these signify the mark of the enemy— Voldemort. Ironically, the good guys also have a mark: the DA coins, which transmit messages to members of Dumbledore's Army throughout the latter half of the series.

666: One of the great mysteries in Revelation is who the Beast that leaves its mark actually is. Scholars have theorized for years about the identity of the Beast, who is known only by the number 666 (Rev. 13:18-19). Some scholars in recent years have suggested that the biblical text refers to the historical figure Nero Caesar, a tyrannical ruler renowned for his persecution of the early Christians, because the letters of his name add to 666 using an ancient practice of assigning numbers to letters in both Greek and Hebrew. Other scholars maintain that this figure has yet to appear in history. While readers don't see letters taking numeric values and adding up to anything in the *Harry Potter* series, it wouldn't be beyond reason to propose that the Tom Riddle/Lord Voldemort acronym is done in the same spirit. Lord Voldemort, like 666, is a symbol that hides the identity of evil's embodiment.

Serpents: Serpents signify evil throughout Revelation and other parts of the Bible. It is therefore fitting that Slytherin's symbol is the snake, the Dark Lord keeps a snake at his side, and a basilisk lives in the Chamber of Secrets.

Defeat and return of Satan: The text of Revelation chapter 20 says that an angel will throw Satan, who takes the form of a dragon or ancient serpent, into a pit for a thousand years. During that time, Christ will reign with martyrs, but at the end of that period, Satan will be released again, and only at that time will permanent defeat occur. This plot is remarkably similar to what happens in the seven *Harry Potter* books: Lily initially defeats Voldemort, but the success isn't permanent. Voldemort is relegated to a bodiless prison, which makes him enfeebled and relatively powerless, as Satan was during his imprisonment. The Dark Lord then finds release from that hiatus in book four, when he regains his body, and eventually this leads to warfare and Voldemort's final defeat.

Possible Objection

There is more than one side to any argument, and suggesting that Rowling's books bear Christian apocalyptic themes is no exception. Perhaps the greatest challenge arises when we consider the role of forgiveness in the series. The concluding chapters of Revelation say that heaven and earth will be made new, but only those who were faithful will be able to enter. The biblical text says that, "Nothing unclean will enter it, nor anyone who practices abomination or falsehood but only those who are written in the Lamb's book of life" (Rev. 21:27). This sentiment is echoed elsewhere in Revelation, as in chapter 20, which says that only those who have not worshipped the Mark of the Beast can reign with Jesus during his thousand-year rule (v. 4). While Revelation is clear that the righteous will receive their reward and the evil their punishment, *Harry Potter* seems to offer a greater possibility of forgiveness and reconciliation with the enemy. Even in his final moments of life, Harry encourages Voldemort to repent, and in the epilogue we see Draco Malfoy standing with his family at Platform 9 ¾. Though Rowling depicted him a sobering manner—he has a receding hairline and does not seem particularly gleeful—it is a far cry from the punishment he could have received had he been subjected to a soul-sucking encounter with Azkaban's dementors. Moreover, the conclusion seems to present the possibility of full reconciliation in the future, holding out the hope that the animosity between the Malfoy family and Harry's friends—between the Death Eaters and Dumbledore's Army— might disappear completely in the future. Hence, Hermione doesn't want to discourage her daughter from prematurely judging Draco's son, telling Ron, "Don't try to turn them against each other before they've even started school!" (*DH*, 756).

Yet there is a foil in this objection: the books may emphasize a strong doctrine of forgiveness that contradicts elements of Revelation. But that doesn't mean that they contradict Scripture at large. On the cross, for instance, Jesus pleads for mercy for his executors, saying, "Father, forgive them; for they do not know what they are doing" (Luke 23:34). Likewise, in the Sermon on the Mount, Jesus reinterprets the Jewish law and says, "You have heard that it was said, 'You shall love your neighbor and hate your enemy.' But I say to you, Love your enemies and pray for those who persecute you, so that you may be children of your Father in heaven; for he makes his sun rise on the evil and on the good, and sends rain on the righteous and on the unrighteous. For if you love those who love you, what reward do you have? Do not even the tax collectors do the same? And if you greet only your brothers and sisters, what more are you doing than others?" (Matt. 5:43-47). Gospel passages like these make a strong case that forgiveness is not antithetical to God's will but rather the hope for all. That the *Harry Potter* books also present a desire for forgiveness makes it more difficult to say that they contradict Scripture.

The second objection one might raise is that there is not literally a new world at the end of the series. Rather, the wizarding world is becoming "new" in the here and now. While this picture contradicts some Christian strains of thought, it reinforces others. Realized eschatology, an idea promoted by Clement H. Dodd at the turn of the twentieth-century, suggests that with God's help a "new heaven and a new earth" can be inaugurated by humans at any time. But humans must take steps to help bring it about. In other words, those who are made in God's image use that image to do God's work in the world. The philosophy of the *Harry Potter* books fits nicely into this framework: when characters adopt love as their motive, they participate in work that transforms the wizarding world from a place of violence and discrimination into one without sorrow, crying, or pain.

The Ending of the End

We talked in other chapters about how the *Harry Potter* books seem to have a kind of keep-it-real attitude that places an emphasis on how God can be discovered in this world. We see this same stress in how the books deal with the end times. A reign of peace may only be accomplished through the power of love—just as God's power enacts a new world from the Christian perspective—but it can only come about when humans agree to help. Only then can love work through others to bring about a more peaceful, accepting global community.

For members of Harry's world, this means that the choices they make matter. Only when they commit to believe in love and then work on its behalf does love have the possibility of trumping evil. But the same might be said of our world as well. Until each person takes on the challenge of living with a generous and loving heart, there is no hope for a world without tears.

This is the message I leave my students with at the close of term: that in the end, the hope for Harry's world is the same as the Christian hope for ours. But it will remain a hope until we live in a way that can make it a reality. I also see, on that final day, that it can be a reality. Students that I worried would never get along because of religious or social differences are now friends. They laugh and smile and support one another. They email each other for advice on papers and ask each other over for dinner. They carry on the tradition of baking for one another—as exemplified by my student who made a cake in the shape of a Snitch for our end year party—and they agree to go to the Harry Potter theme park together. In short, they are good to one another, and I hope they will take that kindness out into the world with them so that for themselves and for others, all will be well.

Questions for Your Reflection

1)   The eschaton is frequently associated with hope. How is hope characterized in the *Harry Potter* series? Think of hope regarding specific situations as well as people who are hopeful.

2)   What is the Babylon of the *Harry Potter* series? In what ways do characters think that Empire has won? In what ways does the rumor of its defeat start? How is this rumor actualized?

3)   In between Lily's defeat of Voldemort and Harry's defeat, how is the end times theme developed? Who treats this time period like a special lapse in an ultimate plan? How do people become aware of it?

4)   Are people judged in the *Harry Potter* series? How does their judging or lack of judging relate with themes from the Book of Revelation and the moment of the cross? How does judgment work in either biblical case?

5)   What do you think about the new world created at the end of the *Harry Potter* series? Is all well? Does this chapter make you feel differently about the epilogue?

Conclusions at the Semester's End

Our own End Times

My students and I met in the courtyard of Branford College for our final meeting. Sitting on the grass, they talked about how sleep-deprived they were from finishing their final papers, and I heard the enthusiasm in their voices when they discussed their summer plans.

Shortly before the end of class, a couple of them disappeared into one of the entryways, re-emerging with a giant box. When they returned to our circle in the grass, everyone grew quiet and one of them took the top off to reveal a handmade two-foot cake in the shape of a Snitch. Then they handed me a card. In it, each of them had written about their experiences in the class. One of them said that religion was an off-limits discussion in her family, and that the course had made the topic comfortable for her. Another wrote,

> To be honest, religion has always been a somewhat compartmentalized part of my life; maybe my family's faith (Catholic) hasn't always seemed totally relevant to my daily life, or even to the religious questions or problems that I've privately wondered about, but your class's introduction to the wonderful world of theology, I think, has made both Catholicism and Christianity in general a lot more—dare I say?—"magical" (or, at the very least, engaging), and opened up a before relatively unexplored area for me.

This student's words got to the heart of why I wanted to teach the Christian Theology and Harry Potter seminar in the first place: to make students as excited about theology's questions as they were about the wizarding world. Because even though I knew *Harry Potter* had drawn them to the class, I hoped that theology kept them there, that the questions that had fascinated generations of thinkers would capture their minds as well.

We devoured the cake—I splurged and ate two pieces—and then our time was up. My students lingered when class time was over, agreed to meet at the Harry Potter theme park one day, and even, to my delight and embarrassment, called themselves members of Danielle's Army. A few of them hugged me goodbye before they left. Most walked out in small groups, once strangers and now friends.

As for me, I was the last person sitting in the courtyard, the last to leave. It was early evening, the time of day when melancholy is apt to set in, and I let my nostalgia take over. I pondered the sad reality that we would never meet together again as a class, and I wondered about the great things my students would do with their lives. I knew that one of them was headed to law school at Cornell, another was moving to China to teach English, a third had secured an apartment in France and planned on marrying her sweetheart there, and a fourth—to my pride and joy—was going to divinity school at Yale.

As for my other students, most of them were underclassman or undecided, with amorphous futures and the world all before them. But I knew that once they found their way, they would make a difference in the world, one that was for the better. I hoped that, over a classy business dinner or a romantic fireside chat, they might laugh and recall the young, sugar-loving instructor who encouraged them to take some time to ponder the big things. And I hoped that their enthusiasm for the class and the friendships they'd formed were signs that I'd done my job well.

We now find ourselves at the same juncture in this book. It is time to bid farewell, for now at least. I hope that you have learned something about the richness of Christianity and the unique take that the *Harry Potter* books have on that tradition. They point to a faith that believes people suffer from sin and evil, but that the life of Jesus of Nazareth is a sign this pain can be transformed. It is a faith that relies on community, cooperation, and commitment for that transformation to occur. These ideas are at the core of Christianity, just as they are at the heart of *Harry Potter*. They encourage people to invest in those things that enrich their lives and the lives of others, all the while trusting in the power of love. In so doing, they will find a treasure, and a place where their hearts can dwell.

Acknowledgments

This book would not be a reality without J.K. Rowling's inspiring writing. It has been a privilege to work with her material, and I hope my analysis has done it justice.

I am grateful to all those who made the Christian Theology and Harry Potter class a reality. It was the first forum for these ideas and the one that gave me confidence to write this book. Kathryn Banakis and Matthew Johnson sat in my attic apartment and helped me craft the initial syllabus. Frank Keil, Cathy Suttle, and other members of the Yale community believed this class could be a success from the very beginning. My students challenged and shaped the way I view *Harry Potter*'s theology, and I feel so blessed to have been surrounded by their energy and intellect.

Without the wisdom of so many Dumbledores in my life, I would never have become a theologian or a writer. I am indebted to them beyond words. Marilyn McCord Adams's logical mind, care, and chocolate chip cookies fashioned me into a theologian. Laura Severt King and Siobhán Garrigan expected students like me to find their own voice and accepted nothing less. Adela Collins, John Hare, and Serene Jones made studying all the intricacies of Christianity into a lifelong passion. Yale Divinity School, the Institute of Sacred Music, and Berkeley Divinity School at Yale offered me the finest theological education and community I could imagine.

This book reached its final form with the help of many committed colleagues and friends. Karen Silberman and Rob Carver kept me on schedule with our weekly writing dates, and their knowledge of Judaism became my personal encyclopedia. Travis Prinzi and John Granger supported this project from start to finish. Connie Neal believed in this project and provided invaluable knowledge of the publishing industry; without them, I wouldn't have had the courage to publish this book. Amanda Kucik, Jane Jeuland, Deborah Meister, Maggi Dawn, John Walton-Burnight and Nikolaus Wandinger offered their theological and biblical expertise. Julie, Quinn, Elle, and Aidan Carlson motivated this book's completion with their support, meals, edits, hugs, cuddles, and smiles. Joshua Williams was research assistant extraordinaire. Carol Wade lent her patience, support, and knowledge to this project, even at three o'clock in the morning. Katherine Kunz, Erica Thomas, Pamela Shier, Sarah Bradley, Alexis Felder, Dawn DeMeo, and Meredith Liebman read drafts, fed me, discussed the joys and frustrations of book writing, made sure I took time off to ride some roller coasters and were, in short, the best friends a girl could have. My dear Eric Hansen, my amazing, fantastic, wonderful husband, never stopped believing in me. He added lightness and laughter to the long and laborious writing process. And finally, Marguerite and Gregory Tumminio introduced me to both God and the *Harry Potter* books. Without the love of religion and literature they instilled in me, these pages would be blank.

Index

Please note that names are alphabetized by first name.

'666' 157-158

Advanced Potion-Making 129
Albus Dumbledore 12-13, 17, 28-38, 50-56, 68-71, 74-75, 83, 86-87, 90, 92, 92-97, 117-122, 126, 129-130, 133, 136-140, 147, 149, 150, 154
Alexandrians 66-67
Antiochians 65-67
Antiochus Epiphanes
Appollinaris
Arius 63-65, 80
atonement 77-78, 81
Anselm of Canterbury 79-80, 87, 96, 112, 184
apocalypticism 126
Athanasius 63-65
Augustine of Hippo 20-23, 26, 37, 42-43, 80, 143-147, 149

Babylonian Exile 152
Bellatrix Lestrange 33, 39, 53, 93, 137, 149, 150
Blaise Pascal 137

Cedric Diggory 9, 90, 92, 97, 98, 106, 150
Charles Wesley 127
Chamber of Secrets 29-30, 32, 129, 158
Christmas 15, 139
Clement H. Dodd 160
Clive Staples (C.S.) Lewis 109-110, 135-136, 143-147, 149, 150
corporate sin (see social sin)
Council of Chalcedon 66-68
Cyril of Alexandria 66
Cyrus the Great 152

CPSIA information can be obtained
at www.ICGtesting.com
Printed in the USA
LVOW12s2356160817
545328LV00001B/12/P